Sermons from Mind and Heart

Sermons from Mind and Heart

Struggling to Preach Theologically

Rodney Wallace Kennedy

WIPF & STOCK · Eugene, Oregon

SERMONS FROM MIND AND HEART
Struggling to Preach Theologically

Copyright © 2011 Rodney Wallace Kennedy. All rights reserved. Except for brief quotations in critical publications or reviews, no part of this book may be reproduced in any manner without prior written permission from the publisher. Write: Permissions, Wipf and Stock Publishers, 199 W. 8th Ave., Suite 3, Eugene, OR 97401.

Wipf & Stock
An Imprint of Wipf and Stock Publishers
199 W. 8th Ave., Suite 3
Eugene, OR 97401
www.wipfandstock.com

ISBN 13: 978-1-61097-263-5

Manufactured in the U.S.A.

All scripture quotations, unless otherwise indicated, are taken from the Holy Bible, New International Version®, NIV®. Copyright ©1973, 1978, 1984 by Biblica, Inc.™ Used by permission of Zondervan. All rights reserved worldwide.

"Otherwise" reprinted by permission of Graywolf Press, Saint Paul, Minnesota, from *Otherwise: New and Selected Poems.* © 1996 by the Estate of Jane Kenyon.

"The Summer Day" reprinted by permission of the Charlotte Sheedy Literary Agency Inc. from *House of Light.* © 1990 by Mary Oliver.

"The Journey" reprinted by permission of Grove/Atlantic Inc., New York, from *Dream Work.* © 1986 by Mary Oliver.

"The Greatest Grandeur" reprinted by permission of Milkweed Editions from *Firekeeper: New and Selected Poems.* © 1994 by Pattiann Rogers.

Contents

Acknowledgments ix
Foreword by Brad J. Kallenberg and William Vance Trollinger xi
Introduction xxi

1. The Church of Water and Fire 1
2. Degrees of Glory 6
3. The Devil Came Down to America 11
4. Is the Gospel Socialist? 16
5. Does Jesus Save? 21
6. May God 'Easter' in Us 27
7. If Seeing is Believing, Faith is Toast 32
8. The Reliable God 37
9. When God Shocks Us 42
10. A Woman's Place 48
11. Understanding Others 53
12. A Christian Remembrance of Those Who Died in War 59
13. Lessons in Praying from the Jews 64
14. Jesus as Trouble 69
15. Worship: A Sunday Choice 73
16. Thanksgiving: Are We Still Pilgrims? 78
17. When the Preacher Is Depressed 84

18 A Christmas Witness 89

19 Would You Like to Hold the Baby? 94

20 Remember Your Baptism 98

21 The World's Savior and America's Prophet:
      Dr. Martin Luther King Jr. Sunday 103

22 Are We Actually Following Jesus? 107

23 How to Be Blessed 112

To the First Baptist Church of Dayton for accepting my habit of believing that a sermon requires space and time that transcends the impatience of our culture.

To Johnelle, first listener to every sermon I write and preach.

To Camron, Emily, Katie, Isaiah, and Cleary, the amazing gift of grandchildren.

Acknowledgments

I NEED TO THANK my wife, Johnelle, for all those Friday and Saturday nights she listened to the first oral delivery of my sermons. She has not only listened with amazing patience and care, she has encouraged, suggested, and at times, simply told me, "I wouldn't say that if I were you." I have argued against her suggestions with passion (after all, one's words are like one's children) and usually made the changes. Most of all, she insisted for years that I submit my sermons for publication. I am also indebted to Maureen Schlangen for all she did to make this book possible. Her editing skill made this transition from the oral to the written word seamless. I would like to thank Brad Kallenberg and Bill Trollinger for their input and their remarkable foreword to this book.

Sermon ideas often form in two lectionary groups that make up part of my weekly practice: the Monday night group of Luann and Tim Meador, Sue and Mark Sawyer, Ed Wingham, Andy Black, Sue and Bill Trollinger, Jeanne and Brad Kallenberg, and Johnelle Kennedy; and the Thursday morning group of Ed Rhodes, Nick Gough, Charlene Bayless, Jule Rastiskis, Jim Earnest, Marilyn Craig, Diane Ashman, and Peggy and David Coggins.

For the past eight years, I have been privileged to serve as pastor of First Baptist Church of Dayton. There is an historic sense of expectation about the sermon built into the Gothic sanctuary. The space speaks, "Preach well, intelligently, and with passion." The space was built under the leadership of a major figure in the Fundamentalist movement of the early twentieth century and is still filled with the spirit of Charles Seasholes, the quintessential 1950s liberal. There is at least some irony that a church founded by rock-ribbed Calvinists now has a full-blown Arminian pastor. The congregation has always insisted that her pastors make the effort to preach well, and the congregation made it possible for me to give so much of my time to the creation of sermons, including a one-month reading sabbatical every year. If ever sermons were the product of preacher and people, this is the case with First Baptist Church of Dayton.

While I believe that sermons mostly have a short shelf life, like a fly that lives gloriously for one day, and that the sermon has trouble inhabiting forms other than the immediate, temporal, and rhetorical, I am amazed at the ongoing conversation of preaching in this congregation. Their love and knowledge make it impossible not to attend to the act of preaching.

Foreword

One does not flip through a car manual and mistake it for poetry. Nor does one pick up the Sunday comics and mistake them for a Physicians Desk Reference. That is because native speakers seldom make mistakes of genre when reading ordinary English texts. Yet pick up a collection of sermons, and one may feel at a loss: What is going on here? What am I to make of *these* sentences? What sort of genre is *this*? What am I, as a reader, to expect (or not to expect) from a *sermon*, especially from a *printed* sermon? Should I expect entertainment, like the comics? Instruction, like the car manual? Inspiration, like the poem? Information, like the Desk Reference?

Ordinary living is generally adequate for schooling readers for shifting effortlessly from novels to phonebooks to newspapers and back again. But unlike bygone eras inhabited by our grandparents and great-grandparents, ordinary living today may *not* sufficiently equip us to read sermons *as sermons*. Our aim in this Foreword is to help you, the reader, to understand the genre of "sermon" in general and to locate this particular batch of sermons in the life of First Baptist Church of Dayton, Ohio in the year 2010.

What then is a sermon? As tempting as it is to approach a sermon as one might an op-ed piece or a longish blog, we claim that it is mistaken to do so. *A sermon is a performative speech act that brings an occasioned, but ongoing conversation to bear upon a canonical text.* This definition is only as clear as are its terms. So, let us unpack them one at a time.

First, a sermon is a "performative speech act." The notion of a "speech act" derives from the work of twentieth-century Ordinary Language philosopher, J. L. Austin. At the time of Austin's work at Oxford, it was widely believed that the most natural use for language was description. Sentences were thought to benignly mirror the world, like a digital photo captures a moment without disturbing the furniture. But that was before Austin slogged through the *entire* Oxford English Dictionary (all eighteen pounds, two thousand four hundred and twenty-four pages of print so tiny that the OED is sold with a magnifying glass!) and catalogued verbs dealing with speaking in order to show that the vast number of speaking verbs have not to do with describing but with *doing something*. (Thus the title of his philosophical work, *How To Do Things with Words*.) He called them "performative" verbs: asking, thanking, greeting, praying, joking, ordering, promising . . . and so on, almost endlessly. Such words do *not* describe states of affairs, but rather *get things done* in our social world. Austin later realized that even "describing" itself is a kind of action; all speech is action and all sentences undertake to perform some work or other. So, by calling a sermon a speech act, we underscore Austin's point that a sermon is an action undertaken. It aims at doing real work.

Second, a sermon involves a conversation. (Austin himself spent a great deal of energy explaining how speaking is like a game of catch—here is the mechanics of the throw, there is flight of the "ball," and then comes the "catch" or uptake by the listener(s). These mechanics need not trouble us here.) By the term "conversation" we do not mean chit-chat about the weather! Rather, we mean something more like the Latin root, *con-verso*, namely, *to go round and round with* or, more colloquially, *to live with*. This implies that a sermon, properly speaking, *cannot* be a unilateral monologue, but rather a moment in the spoken life of a community. As a conversation, the sermon necessarily involves others in the exchange and is only capable of making full sense in light of things spoken both before eleven Sunday morning as well as after.

It is important for understanding this volume to underscore, third, that the conversation called "sermon" is an *ongoing* conversation. In other words, a single sermon is never a self-contained event, or even a riposte within a stand-alone conversation, but a thread in the ongoing tapestry weaving of a community. The very English word, "sermon," owes much to its Latin root, *serere*, which means *to join or link together*. This is the important work that a sermon does: a skillful sermon links persons to persons within a congregation; it links people to their authoritative texts, or "canon"; and it links *this* community (ca. 2010) to *that* community, namely the great cloud of witnesses named in Hebrews 12, a community that extends through the ages, through the present and onwards to the Eschaton. Of course, a given Christian community (like the one at 111 W. Monument Ave., Dayton, Ohio) is never alone in this endeavor to join the historically extended conversation called the Church. Therefore, a skillful sermon links this congregation with all other contemporaneous communities of Christ-followers worldwide. The fact that First Baptist Church of Dayton follows the Revised Common Lectionary is but one small part of our congregation's attempt to "keep in step" (Gal 5:24) with the rhythm and seasons of the Spirit's annual labors in the global Church.

Fourth, a sermon brings an "occasioned but ongoing conversation *to bear upon a canonical text*." This latter phrase indicates that the wide river of theological conversation has its origins in the authoritative voices and texts of Christian Scripture. A primary impetus for keeping the conversation alive is the ever-unfinished business of answering: "What do these canonical texts mean?" and "What, exactly, is the Good displayed therein?" And "What then is human life *for*?" Central to answering these kinds of questions is understanding the scripture as *canonical*. The term "canon" is Greek in origin. It means roughly, "rule" or "metric" or "criterion." As an adjective describing the Bible, the word calls for a distinctive reading strategy. Consider: our scientific age has taught us to *critically* examine texts. We assess a text's argument. We evaluate a text's rhetoric. We judge a text's historicity and veracity and coherence. But notice that in reading critically, we the readers are positioned "over" the text in order to pass judgment on it by means of criteria or metrics derived from somewhere other than the text. In sharp contrast, in reading *canonically*, or approaching a text as canon, the position of readers and text is reversed. Rather than readers being positioned over a text, the text is approached from underneath: a canonical text stands over the readers. Rather than we interrogating the text for its veracity, a canonical reading strategy *invites the text to interrogate us*. The metrics for evaluative judgment are all internal to the canonical scriptures; we—our lives together—are the "text" being scrutinized by the Scripture. Granted, this reversal is counterintuitive because it is countercultural. And therein lies the crucial importance of the sermon: *the sermon is the school in which parishioners learn to read Scripture properly*.

Finally, a sermon is "occasioned." By this term we do not mean that sermons commemorate special occasions like Mother's Day or the Fourth of July. After all, Christians follow the Church's calendar, not Hallmark's. We observe Holy Days, rather than mere holidays. By "occasioned" we mean that sermons are akin to the New Testament Epistles. St. Paul's first letter to the Corinthian church (actually his second letter, but that's another story; see 1 Cor. 5:9) is rightly understood as a letter written by Paul to a particular group in a particular place at a particular time for particular reasons. As we know, social particularities morph over time. Thus the need for additional correspondence (2 Corinthians, etc.). Like the NT letters, the occasioned (or "sited") nature of the sermons contained in this volume require at least a quick sketch of First Baptist Church of Dayton—both its history and the character of the people in the pews—in order to help you as reader imaginatively inhabit the world of these sermons.

The First Baptist Church of Dayton was founded on May 29, 1824—only nineteen years after the city itself was incorporated—by a small band of Calvinist Baptists. After three years of supply pastors, in 1827 the church hired its first regular pastor, D. S. Burnet. The young (nineteen years old at the time of hire!) Burnet was a powerful preacher, and within two years First Baptist membership had jumped from thirteen to eighty-four, making it the largest church in the town (which in 1830 had a population of two thousand, nine hundred fifty). Numerical growth notwithstanding, First Baptist was bucking dramatic changes in the American religious landscape. It was the time of the Second Great Awakening, marked by an emphasis on evangelical revival and fierce opposition to Calvinism. Alexander Campbell was one of the leading figures in the Awakening, and in the wake of his 1829 visit to Cincinnati the Campbellite movement—which emphasized the right of each layperson to read and interpret the Bible for themselves, and which sought to replace denominational "systems" with the New Testament—swept southwest Ohio. First Baptist's D. S. Burnet heard Campbell, was persuaded, and began preaching sermons at odds with the church's statement of faith, in particular the Calvinist doctrine that redemption was only for the elect. Most church members followed Burnet into the Campbellite movement. This majority succeeded in instituting a new statement of faith that substituted the New Testament for the list of doctrines. They were bitterly opposed, however, by eight members who were determined that First Baptist hold fast to Calvinist orthodoxy. For their resistance they were kicked out of the congregation. But while the Campbellite majority departed from the Baptists—and D. S. Burnet became a leading figure in the nascent Disciples of Christ—the "faithful eight" (as they are commemorated to this day on a plaque in First Baptist's foyer) held onto the name of "First Baptist Church of Dayton."

Interestingly, after having paid such a high price for their Calvinism this tiny band of loyal Baptists did not remain rigidly Calvinist. Instead, in the five years after the split they began to incorporate practices more in keeping with the Second Great Awakening, instituting a Sunday School and actively supporting missions. Both Sunday School and missions work were anathema to the hard-core Calvinists who dominated the Miami Valley Baptist Association. As a result, in 1836, the First Baptist Church of Dayton (along with three other Baptist churches in southwest Ohio) was booted from the organization.

But as First Baptist increasingly moderated and eventually abandoned its Calvinist commitments, its numbers grew dramatically (by the late nineteenth century the Sunday School had over seven hundred members) while the hyper-Calvinist churches struggled to survive. This determination to stake out a moderate theological course—better stated, this determination to navigate between theological extremes—sets the pattern for First Baptist's history. And it is not the only way in which the church's early history prefigured what was to come. From the very beginning, with D. S. Burnet, the First Baptist Church of Dayton has prized gifted preachers and strong leaders as senior pastors. This point is underscored by the photos of the First Baptist ministers that currently line the hallway between the sanctuary and the Christian education complex, photos that go all the way back to Burnet (a photo which serves as a telling counterbalance to the plaque in the foyer honoring his opponents).

In the latter part of the nineteenth century that man was Henry Francis Colby, who pastored the church from 1868 to 1902, while also serving as president of the American Baptist Missionary Union, the president (for twenty-two years) of the Board of Trustees of Denison University, and the president of Miami Valley Hospital (nineteen years). Colby cemented a third characteristic of First Baptist, that is, it has always understood itself as playing an important role in the city of Dayton and in the larger church. This was clear in the hiring of J. C. Massee as senior pastor in 1912. Massee had been pastor of First Baptist in Chattanooga since 1908, and in that time the church membership roll had increased by five hundred. More than this, Massee was an internationally renowned evangelist—as First Baptist's pastor he organized a number of revival meetings in Dayton, as well as continuing his larger evangelistic campaigns—who had published two books and had received an honorary doctorate from Mercer University. He assumed the First Baptist pastorate just in time to shepherd the congregation through the building of a new church. Ground was broken just three months before the devastating March, 1913 flood that swept the city, killing three hundred sixty people (and swamping the standing First Baptist building with nine feet of water, as well as the foundation for the new church). But Massee expertly guided First Baptist through the crisis: when the floodwaters abated, and the city had begun to recover, the building resumed. The cornerstone was laid on May 31, 1914; on June 26, 1915 the magnificent Gothic structure opened its doors, the back of the building abutting the Miami River, and its grand entrance—befitting its understanding of its role in the city—proudly facing Dayton's downtown. This beautiful edifice remains the home of First Baptist Church today.

Massee was strongly committed to Biblical inerrancy and dispensational premillennialism. Given his prominence it was not surprising that he was present for the first meeting of the World's Christian Fundamentals Association in Philadelphia in May 1919. Not coincidentally, in 1919 Massee also left First Baptist of Dayton for the more prominent pulpit of Tremont Temple in Boston; from this location he served as one of the major leaders of the emergent fundamentalist movement (although, in keeping with the Calvinists who founded First Baptist, he ended up being excoriated by fundamentalist leaders for not being sufficiently fundamentalist).

One might take from the Massee pastorate—which was clearly a great success—that by the early twentieth century First Baptist Church of Dayton had lined up on the conservative side of the great divide in American Protestantism. But as indicated above, First Baptist has historically resisted affiliating itself with one theological extreme or the other. So but twelve years after Massee left for Boston—in 1931—the church hired Charles Seasholes as senior pastor. With a doctorate from Newton (now Andover Newton) Seminary, Seasholes was a charter member of the Roger Williams Fellowship, a liberal group in the American Baptist Convention that prized diversity of opinion on the denomination, and that was committed to the notion that "the New Testament is the all-sufficient ground of our faith and practice" (which of course D. S. Burnet and the Campbellites proclaimed at First Baptist in 1829, much to the consternation of the "faithful eight"). Seasholes was also very involved in the ecumenical movement, even serving as a delegate to the initial meeting of the World Council of Churches in 1948. At First Baptist Seasholes introduced the practice of ministers and choir wearing robes and organized Wednesday evening lectures on world problems and Sunday evening book review discussions. He served on innumerable city committees and boards, helped bring Planned Parenthood to Dayton, and presided over Orville Wright's funeral in February of 1948.

Charles Seasholes was pastor from 1931 through 1965. He presided over First Baptist's glory years, the memory of which remains strong among some at First Baptist today. Of course, it is no accident that First Baptist's glory years correspond with the decades in which mainline Protestantism dominated American religion; even more to the point for this urban church, the Seasholes years were the same years that Dayton—an industrial powerhouse for the first half of the twentieth century—was booming, with a vibrant downtown and a population of 262,332 in 1960. But corresponding with the fracturing of mainline Protestantism and the hard times besetting Dayton—the 2010 census revealed a population of 141,527 in what is now understood as a "Rust Belt" city—the church endured a time of decline, punctuated by a scandal in the 1990s involving the pastoral staff. By the early years of the twenty-first century the once-glorious First Baptist Church was down to fifteen families rattling around in the large Gothic structure in the middle of a city struggling to survive.

But these families had not surrendered. In 2003 the First Baptist Church of Dayton called Rodney Wallace Kennedy to be senior pastor. Even in its diminished state First Baptist was determined to have strong preaching from the pulpit. It was a masterstroke. A refugee from the fundamentalist-captured Southern Baptist Convention, with a PhD in rhetoric from Louisiana State University, Rod Kennedy fits very well the profile of a First Baptist Church senior pastor. As you will see in the sermons that are to come, he is a fabulous preacher who cannot be—and does not want to be—pegged as liberal or as conservative. More than this, Rod has a prominent local profile, thanks to five books, a blog, and numerous columns in the local newspaper; membership on innumerable community boards and involvement in a variety of civic reform efforts; and, a leadership role at the local United Theological Seminary (which includes the establishment of a Baptist House of Studies) and an ongoing teaching gig at the University of Dayton Lifelong Learning Institute (where his classes attract an outrageous number of loyal students).

Thanks to Rod's preaching and leadership, the work of a dedicated pastoral staff, and a good number of energetic laypersons, in the past ten years worship attendance has risen from the depths to over two hundred on an average Sunday morning (and this while Rod and his colleagues aggressively eschew anything that looks like the stereotypical "church growth" strategy). In keeping with many mainline churches, the congregants are a remarkably diverse lot. Almost the entire theological spectrum is represented (which various folks find disconcerting on one occasion or another). Ditto for the political spectrum: a number of folks are very conservative politically (a few would identify with the Tea Party movement); another group has deep loyalties to Wright Patterson Air Force Base in particular and the military in general; others are theological pacifists and politically liberal or leftist. Economically, there are some wealthy members, which is in keeping with the early twentieth century when First Baptist was perhaps the elite church in Dayton—but this is certainly not the norm. It is fair to say that a good number of professionals attend the church; unlike many Baptist congregations, First Baptist has a good number of MDs and PhDs, as well as a healthy contingent of graduate students from the University of Dayton. Finally, while the church remains quite "white," over the past five years it has started to become more racially diverse.

In keeping with many or most historic downtown congregations, the First Baptist membership is spread across a vast geographical area, thus making it a substantial effort for many members to make the trip to church once a week. During the Kennedy years the church has moved to more liturgical worship (Baptist-style), which includes the use of a common lectionary, but which also includes an invitation at the end of the service. While the Lord's Supper is celebrated once a month, a few years ago an optional communion service was established, held every week after the regular worship service in a small chapel off the sanctuary.

First Baptist is not really a church of "small groups"—unless one counts choir, Sunday School, and the like—and even these activities are understood as voluntary, in the sense that one shows up only if one wants to. Of course, there are "heroic" members—often, but not always, women—who do an enormous amount of labor to make the church run. On the other hand, church members are great givers of money—even in times of economic hardship. Even more striking, virtually everyone pitches in one way or another to do social justice, be it packing sack lunches (six hundred per month) for the homeless, participating in the annual renovation of a poor person's home, attending civic and political rallies, and/or advocating for the various marginalized in the city. Put succinctly, it is striking how many First Baptist members who live outside the city understand that they have a responsibility for Dayton. The church steps still lead directly into downtown.

We hope that the notion of "sermon" is a little clearer: *A sermon is a performative speech act that brings an occasioned, but ongoing conversation to bear upon a canonical text.* As you'll discover, some of the sermons in this volume have an academic feel, complete with footnotes for further study. Others have an impressionistic force that might be compared to the paintings of Monet or the music of Debussy. Some paragraphs are tightly woven philosophical argument. Other paragraphs pile sentences moving in opposite directions on top of each other in ways vaguely akin to poetry. Perhaps the best advice we can offer is that you as reader *work* to imaginatively inhabit 111 West Monument Avenue, Dayton, Ohio, remembering the liturgical season and envisioning your own elbows rubbing with those of fellow worshippers. Then *listen* (more than read) to the Voice that speaks through these sermons.

Brad J. Kallenberg, Associate Professor of Theology
William Vance Trollinger, Jr., Professor of History
The University of Dayton

Introduction

"Damn you, Stanley Hauerwas!" For more than twenty years, I was a comfortable, popular preacher. My concentration was on delivery more than content. My primary concern was the discovery of interesting, fascinating material. Frankly, I was more interested in being humorous than in being faithful to the Gospel. Congregational laughter and praise were my drugs of choice. The research in communication that deplored the deterioration of adult attention span led me to construct sermons designed to inform and entertain. Sermon value was judged on the basis of how much laughter there was during the sermon and how much praise there was after the sermon. Any attempts to read those sermons are now painful and disorienting. I don't recognize the preacher in the words on the page. I deceived myself into believing that I was prophetic because I was against fundamentalism. At no point did I have enough sense to realize that anger is a debilitating taskmaster, not an angel leading to truth.

Then in the summer of 2007, I read Stanley Hauerwas' *The Peaceable Kingdom*. As a matter of fact, with a condition my wife calls "selective obsessive-compulsive disorder," I read every book Hauerwas published. This led to the reading of John Yoder and William McClendon. Since I was schooled in the Anabaptist tradition, had training in Baptist church history, and had read the autobiography and fiction of Anabaptist Will Campbell (*Brother to a Dragonfly* and *The Glad River*), I felt somewhat at home in this material.

Reading has always been my first passion. To credit the authors that nursed me through the hills of North Louisiana and took me places I had never been would be an impossible task. Among those that still stir my soul are Carlyle Marney; Flannery O'Connor, a Catholic Southerner whose flawed Protestant characters were too real in my own life to be labeled caricatures; Pat Conroy, whose *Prince of Tides* left me overjoyed and depressed for at least two weeks and taught me what it means to be a

Southerner; Harry Emerson Fosdick, the Baptist hero in the fight against Fundamentalism—the early twentieth-century version; Aristotle and Plato, my graduate school companions; Balthasar Hubmaier, the Anabaptist who gave me a sacramental understanding of Baptist life but who was unable to abide the nonviolent theology of his own movement; Rowan Williams; the archbishop of Canterbury; the biographers of practically every person worth a biography; the writers of every book ever published on the subject of homiletics, including all of the Lyman Beecher Lectures in Preaching from Yale University; and most important of all, the Holy Bible. I simply couldn't get enough of holy writ. No matter how turned off I was at the ardent, zealous defenders of the Bible's alleged literalism (how boring) and the inerrancy of the imaginary original autographs of all those books that never appeared in one volume until centuries after the last one had been penned, I kept reading the Bible. Every time a new version came out, I purchased a copy and read it straight through. I still read the King James Version, but the New Revised Standard is my favorite version for study. J. B. Phillips got me through college. A copy of the Moffett Translation, picked up at a book fair for fifty cents, still amazes me. Only after getting home did I realize that the fifty-cent price was because sections of the concordance were liberally sprinkled throughout the texts of the various books of the Old and New Testament. No matter, I still like to read this partial copy of the Bible.

To this day, I can't imagine a sermon that doesn't begin in a biblical text. Preaching without the language of the Bible would be as impossible for me as not speaking my native tongue. In fact, I don't know whether I learned to speak Bible or English first. As a veteran of the Bible Memory Drill contests in church, I memorized one hundred verses of Scripture per month.

While I did not come to my initial reading of Hauerwas unprepared, his writings challenged me at levels I did not expect. Again and again, I kept coming back to his writings. There's no way of pinpointing when it happened, but my entire approach to preaching changed. That it did so unconsciously and without my permission still rattles me. The power of one's reading and reading habits instills in a person far more than we can account for in any rational way. For more years than I can count, I have disciplined myself to read one hundred fifty pages a day. Somewhere, I once read that the average Jewish rabbi read six times more than the average Protestant pastor. I copied that quote and kept it on my desk for years. As a poor country boy, I had perfected the art of being motivated by challenges, especially those that suggested I didn't know enough or read enough. Most of all, I am always on the alert for any slight suggesting I wasn't intelligent enough.

None of this, however, prepared me for the impact Hauerwas had on me as a preacher. As I struggled to discover the "church" promoted by Hauerwas, I decided that such a church could only exist if it was visible, actual, and flesh-and-blood. I also felt that a steady diet of preaching rooted in the gospel of peace was a necessity if we were to actually be such a church. My working hypothesis was that a church fed a steady diet of the gospels and the teaching of Stanley Hauerwas would be a different church. The results are not all in, but at every turn I have been surprised, challenged, and at times, scared.

Regardless of the ultimate outcome, I find myself unable to stop this journey. I keep coming back to Hauerwas again and again. Since he claims to have said everything he knows in *The Peaceable Kingdom*, I recently invited my congregation to join me in a line-by-line reading of the work. The response was so underwhelming that I decided that I would preach a series of sermons that included the ideas and themes of *The Peaceable Kingdom* and not tell the congregation what they were hearing. I am in the middle of this subterfuge as I write these words.

One result of this subterfuge—which I call a homiletical experiment: The subjects of peace and violence keep appearing. I talk about violence a lot because our self-deception and our impatience make all of us more violent than we realize. None of this work could be labeled fun, humorous, or entertaining, but I promise you one thing, it is never boring. The ongoing conversation between my mostly unsuspecting congregation and Stanley Hauerwas, my conversation with an unsuspecting Hauerwas, and our steady engagement with large amounts of Scripture may have changed me more than it has the congregation. All I know for sure is that once I was angry, and now I am glad. Once I was self-deceived; now I see persons walking as if they were trees. In my business, that may be called progress. At least I am hopeful.

One particular critique offered by Hauerwas and United Methodist Bishop William Willimon in their work *Resident Aliens: Life in the Christian Colony* is that Baptists had nothing more to go on than the New Testament; now, this really irked me. Hauerwas and Willimon contend that among Baptists, it seems one can only be liberal or fundamentalist with nothing in between. For one thing, I dissent from this view. While I don't doubt whether scholars as brilliant as Hauerwas and Willimon know the Baptist song, I do doubt they know the tune. After all, Hauerwas is a denominational vagabond who has only in recent times landed in the tree of the Episcopal Church (since I am a confirmed Episcopalian and an American Baptist, this is another point of intersection with Hauerwas). I also dissent from this truncated view of Baptist history not because I am insulted, but because it leaves out a distinct minority of Baptists who have a well-developed sacramental theology and a deep commitment to liturgy. I am part of that group of Baptists. While there are various names attached to the group, I usually refer to myself as a catholic baptist. One of my regular courses at the University of Dayton Lifelong Learning Institute is "Why I am a catholic baptist."

So why do I say, "Damn you, Hauerwas"? Well, now I get e-mails of protest from conservative members and liberal members of the congregation I serve as pastor. Both sides are uncomfortable with this gospel of nonviolence that I can't help but proclaim. Both sides accuse me of being political. All I can say is, "So what?" Life is political. Religion is political. To be apolitical would be to stop breathing.

I also am uncomfortable. Growing up addicted to applause and praise from church members encouraging my youthful preaching makes it hard dealing with controversy. Hauerwas and company have shattered some of my self-delusions and put me in a place where I can't help but preach what I have read, seen, and heard. In spite of everything, I could not imagine returning to my previous state. While I may not be fully clothed and in my right mind, I do know that my name is no longer Legion (I have discovered at least part of my own voice), and I am no longer haunted by the demons that caused me to fill my sermons with a quote a minute.

My reading experience of Hauerwas, the most profound and profane person I've ever met, caused me to remember my own history. Growing up a fundamentalist Baptist, I had never been able to find an acceptable way to move from that part of my history without anger or denial. Having discovered that anger is not a good companion in the pulpit, I still didn't know quite how to stop attacking the version of faith I imbibed in my youth. Once I accepted this history, I was able to also accept the powerful biblical memory formed in my heart and mind by my Sunday School teachers and pastor. Hauerwas freed me to embrace my history, and that embrace allowed me to celebrate the virtue and the value of that history. While no one would mistake me for a fundamentalist, I am grateful for the biblical language that echoes in the words I write and speak. Having read the diatribes of a number of ex-fundamentalists, I felt abused. These writers were not free; they had simply changed masters.

In the sermons that follow, I attempt ways to articulate what I believe is my own authentic voice—a voice that has found a third way. I am convinced that this third way is not a compromise and is not encapsulated by the ambiguous term "moderate." So far, I fail in all attempts to find a label. After all, as Kierkegaard put it, "Once you label me, you negate me."

In some sense I dedicate these sermons to the Stanley Hauerwas I have come to know in his books and articles. He first harmed me—my feelings, my attitudes, my safe assumptions—and then blessed me. Yet at some primal level, he continues to tick me off. When the men in my small group gave me a copy of Hauerwas' memoir, *Hannah's Child*, I was miffed once again. As Hauerwas explained his relationship to the story of Hannah's prayer for a child, I felt that my own personal and unique story had been stolen.

My dad had prayed and asked God for a son. In return, my dad promised to give this son to the Lord. No one in my family ever breathed a word about this contract my dad had made with God. When I came forward on a Wednesday night, during the hymn of invitation, to tell the preacher that I believed God was calling me to preach, that prayer, in my dad's eyes, was answered. That night when we came home from church, my dad told me the story of his prayer for the first time. Thinking this was my unique story (self-centeredness has such a small field of vision), I felt I had been robbed by Hauerwas. In fact, I had rarely told the story because in the years that I pretended to be a liberal, the story sounded overly pious.

That brings me to the present moment, where I benefit abundantly from a fundamentalist upbringing, a twenty-year sojourn in the land of Christian liberalism, an overdose of Stanley Hauerwas, and a congregation willing to journey with me. I am still an uncomfortable, heavily challenged Baptist preacher. I have discovered the sheer joy of liturgy, the power of the Anabaptist movement, and the joys of being a catholic-baptist. As I continue to read, study, reflect, and preach, I try to keep an open mind as well as the open hands of gratitude for the gifts of God dropping into my mind and heart from the most unexpected sources.

What I remain through all of this is a preacher. Sure, there are days when I wish I were more of a theologian or a philosopher, and I am both of those within the context of one local Baptist congregation. But the one vocation that remains mine from the time my dad prayed for a son he could give to the ministry, from the time I was in my mother's womb—the one vocation that still matters and still drives me—is that of preacher. Of course I am still haunted by the awful ecstasy of being made a preacher at the age of twelve and paraded through the pulpits of small country Baptist churches in the red-clay hills and piney woods of Louisiana. But I no longer feel the need to murder that twelve-year-old boy who was weak, skinny, and precocious—so weak, skinny, and sickly that the church said, "He'll never amount to anything. Let's make him a preacher." The decision, if that is a correct term, to become a preacher, was the right one.

A WORD ABOUT METHOD

Every Monday morning, I begin again the process that will lead at some point between Thursday night and Sunday morning to a four-page, single-spaced sermon in twelve-point Verdana, based on one or more of the lectionary readings for that Sunday. Over the past eight years, I have written more than three hundred sermon manuscripts. Each one has been edited from five to fifteen times during the week before it was actually preached. The sermons in this volume were selected from that collection—1,200 pages of sermonic effort.

I hesitate to make my sermons available for others to read, not only because I doubt whether anyone will purchase a book of sermons by an unknown Baptist preacher from Dayton, Ohio, but also because a sermon is a temporary, in-the-moment, piece of oratory that has a limited shelf life. I fear that I have unconsciously spoken the words of others and thus have no way of giving appropriate credit. Nothing here is original. I gave up the idea of having an original thought long ago. As Pat Conroy says in *The Lords of Discipline*, the best teachers taught me to steal only the best material. Nothing is worse than a thief who doesn't recognize good homiletical material and so raids the Internet for the thoughtless, weak, and insipid sermonic material that can only sound like an echo when used.

Make of this what you will, but when I step into the pulpit, something happens to me, and it changes me dramatically. I never have known what to call it, so I just say that it is my muse. What happens in the twenty minutes of my sermon I can't always account for or recall. I just know that in some sense, it is a complete outpouring of my mind and heart, packaged as a gift of love to the congregation that trusts me enough to allow me to speak my mind and offer my voice to the multitude of voices that have given witness to the power of the Gospel over the centuries. It is an honor to stand in that line of faithful witnesses and to know that having spoken the words of the sermon, God is responsible for what happens next. So if you have actually read these words, please be gentle and know that you missed almost everything that happens on Sunday morning at the First Baptist Church of Dayton between 11:05 and 11:25 a.m.

A WORD TO PREACHERS

As preachers, we are slaves to words. No other word in our language will suffice to describe the suffering, agonizing, difficult task of stringing together words into phrases and sentences that not only make sense, but enliven the imagination—rebuking the slothful, encouraging the weary, and lifting up the downtrodden. The argument about whether preaching is art or science makes little sense to me. Preaching is a learned craft, and unlike Plato's conclusion in the *Phaedrus*, rhetoric, the father of preaching, is not a technique like cooking. Whenever you hear me say, "writing," please know that I am referring to the craft of producing a sermon. My goal is to improve my ability to write. After all, writing can always be improved. I will often say to my preaching class at United Theological Seminary, "Please help me improve this first draft." How many drafts of a sermon do you compose? I average five drafts per sermon, but at times I do a dozen or more.

I try to write/preach a sermon by saying what's in my heart. A preacher shouldn't write as if afraid of something. The sermon demands that we be brave—nothing more or less. Never write a sermon that sounds like somebody you think you are supposed to be. This is why you should never read someone else's sermon, commentary, or article until you have exhausted your thoughts and put them on paper. If you read others first, you will drown you own voice, and it will never see the light of day. You can't write a sermon worrying that you might get run out of town or strung up by a posse. And you can never know when you have exhausted all the possible thoughts in your mind and heart until you have explored deeply all the caves and caverns of your soul, including those memories that depress you or threaten you. Search for your own words in the darkness and in the light. Do not be afraid.

Under no circumstance should you make the mistake of the drunk who was looking under the light of a street lamp for his car keys. Someone asked, "What are you looking for?"

"My car keys," came back the answer.

"Did you park your car here?" the observer asked.

"No. I parked it out back," the drunk said.

"So why are you looking here?" asked the bystander.

The answer: "Because there is more light here."

There may be more light in the words of others, but those words will put out the fire of your imagination like a hard-driving wintry mix. For the sake of your own soul, write down your own thoughts. I am not interested in what others have said until I know what you say. I will sense the words of the "others" in your journey by listening to the way you say your own words. So start there. Promise me that you will write first your own thoughts.

A great sermon can do whatever it wants. Great sermons invite argument and disagreement, but ignorance doesn't even earn a place at the table when ideas are the subject of dispute. Most of the people listening to you preach will have been Christians for many years, and if your sermon doesn't challenge their cultural assumptions, their tribal prejudices, then you have done nothing for them. Your sermon should be the most authentic rendition of the text you are using that you can produce. Sermons exist for many reasons, but one reason is really important for the sake of your own integrity: They force people to examine every facet of their lives and beliefs.

As non-Catholics we are often unfamiliar with the harmonics of the Mass. Pat Conroy says, "Because I was raised Roman Catholic, I never feared taking any unchaperoned walks through the fields of language. Words lifted me up and filled me with pleasure. I've never met a word I was afraid of, just ones that left me indifferent or that I knew I wouldn't ever put to use. When reading a book, I'll encounter words that please me, goad me into action, make me want to sing a song. I dislike pretentious words, those highfalutin ones with a trust fund and an Ivy

League education. Often they were stillborn in the minds of academics, critics, scientists. They have a tendency to flash their warning lights in the middle of a good sentence."

Pat Conroy recommends the practice of hunting, collecting, and gathering words into a notebook.

"Words call out my name when I need them to make something worthy out of language," he said. I pass along his advice because I have found that it works. He suggests that we enter every word that captures our attention in the notebook. Hunt down every analogy, metaphor, interesting phrase—and write them all in the notebook. One of my favorites was written by Allan Gurganus: "when we are fog on a coffin lid."

By now, someone may ask, "Why haven't there been any comments about prayer?" If you have been frustrated at the absence of prayer from these pages, perhaps you feel somewhat like a college mate of mine. Here's the story: As a student at Louisiana College, in a previous life, I participated in a chapel service where the guest speaker was a Baptist historian. The occasion was Baptist Heritage Week, and he was giving a fascinating lecture on the chaotic world of Baptist life. In the middle of his chapel lecture, an acquaintance of mine stood up, waved his hands in the air, and pompously yelled, "Excuse me sir. Could you please say something about Jesus?" After chapel, I pushed him (gently) against the wall and said, "Don't ever embarrass a guest. It's bad manners."

For many years, I felt like prayer was a waste of time. This almost complete disconnect from the primary source of power and wisdom turned my preaching work almost entirely into . . . well . . . my work. I found prayer boring, and I was impatient to get to the office. The discipline of prayer never has come easy for me. Then a friend introduced me to Evening Prayer from *The Book of Common Prayer*. Suddenly, prayer had a structure—a structure I desperately needed. Words came alive on the page. Time spent in prayer wasn't wasted but was now precious. Gradually, under the tutelage of a book of prayer, I learned the value of praying. Sermon work, I now know, requires prayer. Whether I find every prayer time uplifting is of little consequence. What matters is the practice of prayer.

Prayerfully then, I submit these sermons as public documents of my deepest convictions. These sermons are rooted in my mind and my heart, and I offer them to you as an invitation to tell me how they could be stronger and more effective.

1

The Church of Water and Fire

January 10, 2010

Isaiah 43:1–7; Luke 3:15–17, 21–22

Once in my life, I had the privilege of helping name a church. Our group considered hundreds of possible names. During the process, I collected what I considered worst names for a church: Country Club Methodist Church, Sardis Baptist Church (recall Sardis is the dead church in the book of Revelation), and Cold Water Baptist Church. (Cold water: Could this mean that every idea that pastor suggested, the deacons poured cold water on it?)

I want to give our church a figurative name that I pray will be reality for us: The church of water and fire. I want to talk about the challenge of being a church of power in a world that believes the church is irrelevant, meaningless, and harmless. In doing so, let's concentrate on today's readings from Isaiah and Luke.

But first, we need to consider two kinds of religion that hinder our ability to be a church of power—a church of water and fire.

SILLY RELIGION

One kind of religion is what I call "silly religion." There's a lot of silly religion in America today. This is a religion where church is a religious circus, a Texas river, a mile wide and six inches deep, a sideshow in a busy schedule. According to the Barna Research Group, we Americans use the word "God" loosely and often: God is the total realization of human potential, "a higher state of human consciousness," or "everyone is God." Superficial religion offers people what they already believe. It props up the prejudices, biases, assumptions, and politics that church members already have.

Alasdair MacIntyre describes this as "the aftermath of a defeated tradition." The Jesus of silly religion makes everyone happier, wealthier, and of course more successful. Silly religion is handy but it is not big on holiness. It works great in good times—but not so well in a recession.

SCARY RELIGION

Then there is scary religion. Some of us grew up in scary religion. The god of scary religion smells of fire and brimstone. Listening to the sermonic offerings of the preachers of fear, of doom and gloom, takes a certain cast-iron skillet constitution. Even as a child, I noticed that the grown ups didn't seem all that agitated by the preacher's antics. The god of scary religion suffers from a serious need to interfere and mind everyone's business. There's mostly guilt, judgment, denial, and anger. Scary religion beats up people every Sunday and hammers away at the last vestiges of their self-esteem by telling them that they are dirty, rotten sinners. Scary religion has given birth to scary politics, and a cadre of fear-producers populates our pulpits, our talk shows, and our political landscape. And the really scary thing about scary religion: It is thriving, not just among Christians, but among Jews and Muslims as well. Scary religion gives birth to crusades, jihad, hate groups, and terrorists. Scary religion brings out the worst in religion and makes people of faith easy targets for agnostics and atheists.

Well, Isaiah is not interested in silly or scary religion. His congregation is in exile and will be for another 100 years. Languishing in lament in the slave pens of Babylon is not conducive to silliness. For Isaiah, everything is about God: I am the Lord who created you, who formed you: "your Redeemer, the Holy One of Israel."

Isaiah says that life itself is scary enough on its own, and the road home to Jerusalem will be an awful obstacle course. The way out of captivity is as a people. If there is one thing I want us to be intentional about, it is becoming more of a people—a community of faith—a team that works together for one overwhelming purpose.

Isaiah's message is the opposite of the message of scary religion: "Do not fear." Isaiah tells his people their children will go home again. One of my favorite actors, Gene Hackman, co-stars in the movie *Behind Enemy*

Lines. Somewhere inside Bosnia, one of his pilots has been downed, and Hackman says, "Let's go and get our boy back." What a great line—but God outperforms with these words: "Bring my sons from far away and my daughters from the ends of the earth." In the movie, Hackman stands up to NATO; God stands up to the oppressors, the users and abusers of an evil world. He says, "Give me back my sons and daughters."

Our work is to leave our children a church of sustaining, redeeming, and saving power. I am calling this the church of water and fire—the church that evolves out of the common journey: the challenges, the failures, the pains, and the struggles of life and a stubborn faith in God, the Holy One. Silly religion doesn't have the stamina, the seriousness, the soberness to sustain a journey through floods and fires. It is time for the church to realize our task is more like a marathon than a meeting. It's like climbing Mount Everest, swimming the English Channel . . . U.S. troops in the barren mountain terrain of Afghanistan.

So let us consider the alternatives to silly and scary religion.

The church of water: Isaiah recalls for his captured people the memory of the Israelites skedaddling out of Egypt and the Egyptians catching up and cornering them at the Red Sea. Moses said, "Do not be afraid, stand firm, and see the deliverance of the Lord." Isaiah tells his depressed congregation, enslaved in Babylon: One day, God is going to bring you up out of this place. When you have nowhere to turn, nowhere to go, when you think you are down to fate or luck, behold, the Lord will fight for you. You will pass through the water on dry ground.

And in Luke, the baptism of Jesus is a passing through the water. Baptism, you see, changes everything. You are no longer attending church as a harmless cultural experience but as a holiness-producing experience. Baptism, for Jesus and his followers, leads from the waters of the Jordan to a cross on Calvary. It is all one event. Baptism is not only a dipping under water but a lifetime of devotion. The church of water is a gathering of witnesses—potential martyrs. And these faithful martyrs are the exact opposite of suicide bombers. Suicide bombers blow themselves up in the name of their god and kill not only themselves but innocent men, women, and children. In contrast, a martyr's only weapon is the faithful proclaiming of the message of forgiveness and salvation. When demanded to deny faith in Christ, these faithful ones choose death rather than disgrace. Through the martyrs, the faith lives, and people live.

OTHER KINDS OF BAPTISM

There are other kinds of baptism. Devastating experiences are likely to be part of the fabric of our lives: illness, disease, death, loss, divorce. In tough times, we need a tough god and a tough faith. Isaiah doesn't say that God will eliminate the water or the floods. He says that God promises to be with us in the floods. In the church of water, we may at times be overwhelmed but not overcome, knocked down but not knocked out.

Then there is the church of fire. John says, "[Jesus] will baptize you with the Holy Spirit and fire. The chaff he will burn with unquenchable fire." Isaiah says, "When you walk through the fire you shall not be burned, and the flame shall not consume you." Memory is a powerful and appealing part of our lives. One of the best parts of the holidays is sitting together at a fine meal and recalling experiences we had together. Well, Isaiah motivates his congregation with memory. He recalls three Israeli boys in the clutches of King Nebuchadnezzar. Shadrach, Meshach, and Abednego were bound and thrown in the furnace of blazing fire. And as the king watched, he saw four men unbound, walking in the middle of the fire. The king called out, "Shadrach, Meshach, and Abednego, servants of the Most High God, come out of the fire! Come here!" And everyone saw that the hair of their heads was not singed. Isaiah tells his people that the same Lord walking in the fire with Shadrach, Meshach, and Abednego is now walking with them through the fires of oppression, slavery, and humiliation. Memory is a powerful thing, especially memory of the great acts of Almighty God. But the presence of God is not only memory; it is also reality. Walk through the fires of death, and God is there with you.

It is possible that we, suffering from amnesia when it comes to God, have attached our stars to that which is chaff. We have given ultimate meaning to that which is chaff. Luke tells us that God is going to burn away the chaff. A noted theologian suggests that hell is that experience where God burns away the chaff and that, depending on how evil and wicked a person has been, this time of burning away the chaff will last a short time or for many years, but ultimately, everyone will be saved and go to heaven. This would suggest that God will burn away the chaff of our greedy ways. Those who work all the time, with little time for family and no time for God, will have to have the chaff of workaholism burned away. Heaven is all about worship of the divine, not working for dollars.

Someone who lives a life of holiness, a life of commitment to God, will not pass through the fires of hell at all, but be at home with the Lord.

THE HOLY SPIRIT

In the New Testament, this fire is also known as the Holy Spirit. This fire of the Holy Spirit—whatever it is, and however it works—we all need more of it. We must make room for the free, unhindered movement of the Holy Spirit. The Holy Spirit sets our hearts on fire, puts butterflies in our stomachs, makes us lose sleep, makes us breathless with anticipation and stirs our hearts to emotion, passion, and zeal. The Holy Spirit passes out the gifts of administration, leadership, and generosity to some members for the good of all. The Holy Spirit inspires us to give everything to God, up to and including our lives. It is this Spirit that we need more of if we are going to be a church of fire.

Let us not be interested in superficial religion or scary religion. Let us be interested in true religion, in living together as a community. It's about the living God of creation, the life, death, and resurrection of Jesus. It's all about worship. It's about being joint heirs with Jesus, which means everything God gives to Jesus, he gives to us. It's about trusting that God the judge will take everything we have put wrong in the world and in the end make it right. It's about being made perfect in love and being a place for those whose hearts ache for God. That means that every moment we spend together matters as part of our preparation to face a tough and demanding world—from the greeting in the name of our Lord and Savior Jesus Christ to the reading of Scripture to the saying of prayers to the taking of the offering, from the passing of the peace to the singing of hymns. Every little thing we do is preparation for the challenge. You are being asked to join a people, a process, and a journey in holiness and hopefulness and faithfulness to God—Father, Son, and Holy Spirit.

You have come to a place determined to be a city of the living God, a faithful gathering of priests, a church that combines heart and head—a church of water and fire, where the creative power of the Father, the redeeming power of the Son, and the sanctifying power of the Holy Spirit reign forever and ever. Amen.

2

Degrees of Glory

FEBRUARY 14, 2010

*Exodus 34:29–35; 2 Corinthians 3:12–4:2;
Luke 9:28–36 (37–43a)*

LET'S TALK ABOUT GLORY and terror. You have heard it said, "The devil is in the details." Let's change that to say, "The truth is in the details." Like CSI agents, let's dig around in the details until we discover the truth.

Detail: Jesus went up on the mountain to pray. The pattern of the story is that of Christian worship. The transfiguration is surrounded by prayer and Scripture: Moses and Elijah. We have words associated with prayer and preaching, along with words instructing us to listen to Jesus. So understand transfiguration as the church at worship. This is intense because only worship like this can handle the terror that is coming. Jesus is 30 years old—incredibly young—and facing death. That's why there's so much light on this mountain. It will take this much light to penetrate all the darkness of the coming days. Some scholars think this a misplaced resurrection story, but it belongs here. This is worship in the face of terror. Sometimes the glory is born in the grind of daily tasks: praying, studying, and learning the teachings of Jesus. No grind, no glory.

Detail: Jesus glows. He's going to need that glow when the empire tries to extinguish it on Calvary, but Caesar didn't know that the glow came from within: The heart of Jesus glowed with the light of the world. All the arrayed evil in the universe can't put out the light of God. Have you ever noticed how ancient artists painted the face of Jesus shining and glowing? They were trying to say, "This man was raised from the dead." After all, a person raised from the dead is different. No glow, no glory.

And, as the Gospels tell us, in some sense, Jesus glowed because people were attracted to him. The New Testament word for this kind of glow: *kalos.* The root meaning is handsome, gracious, fair to look upon. The Christian life is to be attractive to others. The Christian life is to be a life of lovely goodness. William Barclay calls it winsome beauty. No goodness, no glory.

Don't be skeptical about the glow. Glowing faces shouldn't surprise us: People say that expectant mothers glow. Children at Christmas glow with anticipation. Parents at the announcement of a scholarship glow. Parents at the graduation of their children—glowing. (Grooms? Well, they look terrified.)

Detail: The clothes of Jesus became radiantly white. Transfiguration is tied to the baptism of Jesus. When Jesus had been baptized and was praying, the heavens opened, and a voice declared, "You are my son, the beloved." Maybe Jesus needed to hear the assurance of the father again. And I'm sure you have heard that the early church gave a new white robe to converts as they came up out of the baptismal water. "Clothe yourselves with compassion, kindness, humility, meekness, patience. . . . love. Let the peace of Christ rule in your hearts. And be thankful. Let the word of Christ dwell in you richly" (Colossians 3:12–17).

Detail: And there appeared Moses and Elijah. Three gathered together to discuss death and life beyond death. Now, this is a doctoral seminar for the ages: "How to Die for the World." Or this is a jazz funeral in New Orleans with brass horns and beating drums and twisting and turning this way and that. God bless, they have parades about everything—funerals, Mardi Gras, the saints. Moses and Elijah talk to Jesus about his *exodos,* Greek for his crossing over. Now, here's a powerful thought: Exodus is a coming up out of the land of slavery and being set free. Paul says, "Where the Spirit of the Lord is, there is freedom." And there is life. Even if Moses and Elijah aren't there in person and stand for the law and the prophets—the Old Testament—there's mighty power here. Since the church has a word for death—resurrection—we should have more to say to one another about death. After all, the conversation with the doctor can be terrifying: "It's malignant." "You need open heart surgery." "You have about six months." So see Jesus, Moses, and Elijah talking about passing over to glory on the other side of terror.

Detail: Peter wants to make a monument out of the moment. Of all things, Peter blurts out, "Let's build three tents." High spiritual experiences are transitional and immediate. They don't stay; it's like trying to nail Jell-o to a tree if we try to keep them. Lord knows we have trouble resisting the temptation to build monuments to our own glory: The Burj Khalifa in Dubai, to date the tallest building in the world and nicknamed the Tower of Babel, is 2,720 feet tall. Make no mistake: Peter's first error was idolatry.

In Will Campbell's novel *The Glad River*, Model T takes his best friends Doops and Smilie to a place deep in the Louisiana swamps. He claims no one has ever been there except him. There was a waterfall emptying into a deep pool. Directly across from where the water fell into the pool . . . stood a human-sized cypress knee — a perfect Madonna.

"How do you know nobody has ever been here before?" Doops asked.

Model T said, "We are in the middle of Catholic country. I mean, it's a big thing with us, religion. There are businesses in every little town that do nothing but make statues out of cement. Now, if somebody else had been here, anybody, one of two things would have happened. Either they would have cut it down with a crosscut saw and hauled it out of this swamp by sundown or else they would have slapped down a concrete road where that bayou is and they'd be charging folks a dollar a head just to come in here and see it. Man, believe me, this place would be a shrine by now, and folks would be pouring in here from everywhere. I mean, just look at it!"

"I guess so," Doops said. "But what if one of my people [a Baptist] had found it. We don't pray to statues." Now, the first time Model T had been there he had taken a silver dollar, drilled a hole in it and hung it around the Madonna's neck. "[A Baptist] would have grabbed my dollar," Model T said.

Detail: A voice from heaven corrects Peter's mistake: "This is my Son. Listen to him." Peter's second error was to equate Jesus with Moses and Elijah: one tent for each of them. There are plenty of religious conversations we can have about Jesus, all kinds of validity for the scholarly search for the real Jesus, but there is one unmistakable claim in the Gospels: Jesus is the Son of God.

Now, take one more look at what happened on the mountain. Detail: Peter, James, and John were terrified as they entered the cloud. They are part of a moment where God comes as close to humanity as God ever comes and where humans come as close to God as humanly possible. Of course it's terrifying: We are looking at the destiny of humankind. Everything God has ever done is wrapped up in this Jesus, and the eternal voice of God blesses Jesus to the ministry unto death and life again. This is God's purpose: that we go from glory to glory. God doesn't intend for us to waste our lives deceived by life's pleasures or its sorrows. God expects us to be transformed from one degree of glory to another—to be decisively, eternally conscious of ourselves as destined to participate in the glory of God and to be aware that this God has come to us in the person of Jesus. God doesn't intend for us to live and die in despair but to live from glory to glory (Soren Kierkegaard).

Since we are called to progressive glory, do we see that we can't just go to church on Sunday? When Jesus transfigures you and me, he calls us to extend ourselves, to go deeper into our own faith —deeper into understanding the other denominations, other faiths, other theologies, and other points of view; deeper into engagement with the world for its good.

Extending ourselves beyond the same old things will require of us something like a transfiguration. The economist and philosopher Robert Heilbroner defined inertia as "doing just that thing you know how to do." The church needs to break the inertia created by poisonous politics, disastrous social issues debates, and the violence of religious war. Since we can't do all of it, let me suggest two practical ways that we can help break the habit of just "doing the thing we know to do" and thus extend ourselves.

At some point, the churches are going to have to find a way to live in creative tension with their disagreements, or they are going to have to take a vote and declare the winners. It is a black mark against our faith that we are often incapable of having dialogue about difficult subjects.

We need to move beyond our often-terrible histories and misunderstandings and shift from suspicion, confrontation, and conflict toward trust, conversation, and collaboration, even as we acknowledge our real differences. I want this church to extend the olive branch to all the Christians who are fighting and invite them into serious dialogue about every social issue that threatens to destroy the mainline churches. Let this church be where people of deeply held convictions can openly and respectfully voice those convictions without fear of condemnation.

My second practical appeal has to do with interfaith dialogue. We live in dangerous times made more dangerous by the inability of

Christians, Jews, and Muslims to solve our problems in ways other than war. Let us come together and read our different scriptures together.

Sometimes, people come to church on Sunday carrying their fears, some small and some not so small. We come here with large troubles and the fear that God won't be big enough or powerful enough to help us. We come trying to deny the knot in the stomach and the agonizing despair in the heart, but it's still there. But at church we can extend ourselves beyond the terror. Jesus comes alongside us in our fears and raises us up to behold the glory of God. On the other side of the terror is the resurrected and glorified Jesus. On the other side of the darkness, there is the light of the world. On the other side of the Jordan, there is a band of angels. On the other side of death, there is the hand of Jesus extended to take us home to an eternal glory.

So there's nothing else to do but follow him to glory. Pray like we have never prayed before. Listen to the word from God as if we have never heard it before. Feel the glow of the Spirit in your heart and on your face. Go with God from one degree of glory to another. May God give you glory!

SOURCES

Will Campbell, *The Glad River*

Clyde Edgerton, *Raney*

Soren Kierkegaard, *Either/Or*

Robert Heilbroner

Fred Craddock, *The Cherry Log Sermons.*

Sacra Pagina: Ephesians and Colossians

Sacra Pagina: The Gospel According to Luke

The Anchor Bible: The Gospel According to Luke

David Buttrick, *Homiletic*

Rowan Williams, "A Common Word for the Common Good"

David F. Ford, "Seeking Muslim, Christian and Jewish Wisdom in the Fifteenth, Twenty-first and Fifty-eighth Centuries: A Muscat Manifesto"

Peter Vardy, *An Introduction to Kierkegaard*

3

The Devil Came Down to America

February 21, 2010

Luke 4:1–13

Say the word "temptation," and it triggers giggles. Say the word "temptation," and people remember cute quotes:

- Mae West: "I generally avoid temptation unless I can't resist it."
- Robert Orben: "Most people would like to be delivered from temptation but would like it to keep in touch."
- Facing the dessert cart at a fancy restaurant: key lime pie, crème brulee, chocolate pecan pie, and strawberry pie: "Let's split it."

We talk chocolate fudge and little white lies. Or obsess over sex. These days almost no one (especially the churches) can resist thinking and talking and arguing about sex, especially the sexual peccadilloes of powerful politicians and professional athletes. I grow tired of hearing about the latest high-profile politicians, actors, and athletes caught in transgressions. Here in God's country, we seem to talk about sex in order to hide our propensity for anger, hatred, and increasing apocalyptic violence.

Don't you see this is mere entry-level temptation—the temptation of our so-called lower nature. William Sloane Coffin said, "One of the dumbest ideas that people have ever come up with is the notion that evil arises in our so-called lower nature."

But when we get around to taking seriously the nature of temptation, when we look at Jesus alone in the wilderness, we become aware that temptation is something altogether different from our garden-variety temptations; it's life or death. I have some theological and biblical reflection on the subject, and then we can apply it in a very specific area of thought and action.

A theological word about Satan: Satan is not another deity, opposite God. But Satan is very real, and evil is real. The Satan we meet in the Bible is perceived as a "fallen angel." This tells us that temptation isn't whispering in the ear of Jesus, "Do you want to live like the devil?" The devil doesn't offer Jesus peanut M&Ms or a night out on the town.

With Jesus, temptation asks, "Do you want to be like God?" Be like God, and command stones into bread. Be like God, and rule the world. Be like God, and jump down from the pinnacle of the temple and prove your divinity by being saved by an angelic rescue squad. In the Garden of Eden, the stand-in for Satan, the wily serpent, offered Adam and Eve a piece of delectable fruit as a front while the hidden agenda, the temptation inside the fruit, the worm that would infect the hardware of humanity forever, was, "Do you want to be like God?"

So in the wilderness, Jesus faces Satan's old playbook. Since it worked so well on the first Adam, why change strategy now? Surely the second Adam would possess the same flaw, the same fawning desire to be as God and rule the world.

A theological consideration may help us here: Since there are always a few Gnostics in any Baptist gathering, let me say that the temptation of Jesus was not a piece of fakery. It could have gone the other way. For a long time, the church engaged in theological debate: "Was Jesus ever really tempted?" One group says: *Non posse pecare* – Jesus was not able to sin; the other group says: *Posse no pecare* – he was able not to sin. Let's cut through this debate and say that if Jesus wasn't really tempted, then he wasn't really human. And if Jesus wasn't really tempted, then this story is make-believe. So for the Gnostics, I want to say as clearly as possible: Jesus was truly and completely human. And the testimony of the writer of Hebrews sticks with me as the ring of truth: Jesus, just like us, was tempted in every way, but he did not sin. He could have lived and died as a benevolent emperor, on an earthly throne, but he suffered and died for all.

But the temptations are not over. Let me throw in a little Scriptural teaching for you to consider: Scripture records that Satan left Jesus for a season. Evil, like old heresies we thought were dead and gone, comes back again and again. There's Peter, Jesus' right-hand man, insisting that Jesus abandon all talk of the cross, but Jesus cries, "Get away from me, Satan!" There's the tempter in the Garden of Gethsemane, mentally torturing Jesus with the idea that death on a cross is a cup filled with poison, but Jesus prays that gut-wrenching prayer, "Not my will, but thine be done." There's the tempter firing up the crowd (a satanic specialty is firing up crowds to sarcasm, hatred, and violence) gathered at the foot of the cross. To a dying Jesus, they chant, "If you are really the Son of God, come down from the cross and save us and yourself."

And even more to the point, the temptation is not over to this day. Let's concentrate on temptation No. 2: the offer of all the kingdoms of the world, of complete political control. This temptation concerns me because I think this is where our nation finds itself. In a world where more and more Americans are turning to the presumption of violence—whether as acts of terrorism, mass shootings, hatred of others, or fiery rhetoric about starting an armed revolution in America—we need to pay more attention. In Indiana, Richard Beheny, a Senate candidate, told Tea Party supporters what he would do if the 2010 elections did not produce results to his liking: "I'm cleaning my guns and getting ready for the big show. And I'm serious about that, and I bet you are, too." There's a group called Oath Keepers, whose members call themselves "Guardians of the Republic." They recruit military and law enforcement officers who vow to disobey orders the group deems unconstitutional. The fringe is moving to the center of America. The John Birch Society and the KKK are having growth spurts. The militia groups are intensifying. Greg Evensen, a militia movement leader, has written an article, "The Anatomy of an American Revolution," that details the grievances that would justify a declaration of war against our government. And in case you think this is just an isolated example from the fringe, consider the testimony of Pam Stout, a sixty-seven-year-old housewife from Idaho. She says she is considering the possibility of another "civil war" in America. "Peaceful means," she said, "are the best way of going about it. But sometimes you are not given a choice."

Well, the devil has come down to the United States, looking for a country to steal and destroy. And the temptation is mixed with religion, patriotism, lust for political power, and paranoia. Make no mistake, Satan's offer of power and authority over the kingdoms of the world is as clear a statement as Scripture can make that imperialism and despotism are of the devil.

And it is the church that must stand against the violence. We cannot curtsy in the direction of the Prince of Peace and then go about our violent ways. I'm serious that the church must stop trying to be relevant and trying to reach people on their own ridiculous list of needs, and go back to preaching the radical teachings of Jesus. The hypocrisy must cease. The church can do better. The church must do better. It is the church that must have the prophetic nerve to say no to the notion of teaching that our salvation will come through violent means. It is the Church that must say no even if its own members rise up in rebellion. It is the church that must take seriously pacifism and just war and keep both in the national conversation. The church is called to imitate Jesus. John Howard Yoder, a Mennonite theologian, claims that we are called to imitate Jesus in only one realm, and that is servanthood over dominion, forgiveness over hostility.

As a part-time student of Baptist history, I am convinced that some of our deepest Baptist roots are tied to the DNA of the Anabaptists. In Will Campbell's novel *The Glad River*, Doops explains to a district attorney that the Anabaptists were different: "They did not believe in baptizing infants. They did not believe in taking human life, and would not go to war. They did not believe in the death penalty, so they were not allowed to serve on juries. They believed that the Church and State should be completely separate. They would not swear, because they understood the scripture to forbid it. They led simple lives, did not engage in politics. And a few of them, practiced community of goods."

Doops spends years looking for some Baptists that were like those 16th century Anabaptists. At last, he finds a real Baptist: A Cajun Catholic named Model T. When Model T is executed for a murder he did not commit, Smilie and Doops take him deep into the Louisiana swamp and sink Model T and his coffin into the deep pool of water that had always served as a refuge for Model T. As the casket slipped beneath the cold, clear water, Doops screamed, "Model T the Baptist!" If you are ever confused about how I really think and feel, try to remember that I am more like Doops and Model T than most of the Baptists today.

Plenty of Baptists believe that violence has saving, redeeming power. This is, of course, the very idea that Jesus refuses in the temptations, refutes in his life and sacrificial death, and overcomes in his resurrection from the dead. I don't expect, even in twenty years of preaching, to convert you to the ways of peace, but I am praying that at least half of you will at some point feel guilty about supporting war and atonement through violence. And I'm praying that you will come to see that I'm not trying to make you Roman Catholic; I'm trying to make actual Baptists out of you.

Ask yourself: What if democracy and militarized empire are incompatible? Among the voices clamoring for violence and vengeance, there are other voices. The Founding Fathers saw war as a serious threat to democracy. George Washington disbanded the army after assuming the presidency. In the 1950s, President Eisenhower warned against further development of a military-industrial complex.

Martin Luther King said, "Returning violence for violence multiplies violence, adding deeper darkness to a night already devoid of stars. Darkness cannot drive out darkness; only light can do that." Pope John Paul II: "War should belong to the tragic past, to history; it should find no place on humanity's agenda for the future." The theologian and ethicist Stanley Hauerwas: "Christians do not choose nonviolence because we can rid the world of war, but rather in a world of war we cannot be anything but nonviolent as worshipful followers of Jesus the Christ." Rowan Williams: The idea of a war on terror is as absurd as the war on drugs. John Milbank: There can be no just war against terrorists; they are criminals.

So what can we do? Well, perhaps a little peacemaking. We can try to find ways to promote peace as a foil to the temptations of the devil. We can't promote peace while promoting the illusion that violence is redemptive. We can't promote peace while pretending we are conducting the war on terrorism, when there is no such thing as a just war against a band of thugs and criminals. We can, though, keep resisting the pull of violence and revenge. We can reject the American mythology of violent revenge. We can wage peace in Jesus's name as the cause of our lives. And we can pray the Lord's Prayer every day. The Lord's Prayer is a prophetic apocalyptic prayer and thus is a reality-making prayer, a prophetic speech act. While the violent apocalyptic movement roars, we pray with boldness the prayer Jesus taught us to pray. Jesus prayed victory over temptation into being.

May the strong voice of Jesus be heard over the maddening cries for violence: "My peace I give you. Do not let your hearts be troubled, and do not let them be afraid."

4

Is the Gospel Socialist?

March 21, 2010

John 12:1–8

A Baptist preacher was called to his first church. The chairman of the deacons warned the preacher in advance that several topics were taboo. "Pastor," he said, "don't preach about evangelism, because most of our members don't like that word. And pastor, it wouldn't be a good idea to speak about sin, because many of our congregants think that is old-fashioned. And whatever you do, don't discuss social action since so many people have different political views and might be offended by these issues." So the young preacher asked the deacon, "What should I preach?" The deacon responded, "Why, that's easy—preach the Gospel, of course."

Preach the Gospel? But the church is not of a single mind about the Gospel. Is the Gospel socialist? First let me give the answer: No. The Gospel is not socialist; the Gospel has a heart for the poor. Jesus said, "Blessed are the poor," centuries before Karl Marx cast his bleak shadow across Russia. Instead of putting down the poor, the Gospel lifts them up. Mary, the mother of Jesus, said: "He has put down the mighty from their thrones, and exalted those of low degree; he has filled the hungry with good things, and the rich he has sent empty away." When Jesus preached his first sermon, he said, "The Spirit of the Lord has anointed me to preach good news to the poor." In his signature Sermon on the Mount, Jesus declared, "Blessed are you who are poor, for yours is the kingdom of God." And again and again in his parables, Jesus condemned the economic injustice of this world. He told a story where people who worked one hour were paid the same as people who worked all day. The kingdom of God is not a bottom-line affair. It's all generosity—unconditional generosity rooted in the love of God.

So since our teaching about caring for the poor gets us accused of being socialist, let's take a look at poverty: 37 million Americans live in poverty. More women are poor than men. Why focus on women? The feminization of poverty is a global phenomenon: 77 million girls have dropped out of school, compared to 52 million boys. Women perform two-thirds of the world's work, earn one-tenth of the world's income, are two-thirds of the world's illiterate, and own less than a hundredth of the world's property. These are the residual results of centuries of oppression and mistreatment.

Why does poverty exist in our world? Some say it is systemic, a result of centuries of feudalism, empire, and royalty that centralized wealth in the hands of the few. Some people say that poverty exists because of scarcity: People do not have enough of this world's goods. The solution in this scenario is to give people more. Others see poverty as sin. If your political ideology tends toward the right, you will locate the sin in the poor people. You will argue that they are poor because they are sinful, wicked, lazy, and lacking in ambition. If your political ideology leans to the left, you will locate the sin in corporations, political systems, and a culture of exploitation. For clarity's sake, let's admit that Democratic attempts to eliminate poverty have often ended in disaster and have perpetuated generations of dependency relationships. And Republicans have made little effort to address poverty. By and large, their approach has been that a prosperous rich class will allow enough money to filter down to eventually help the poor. Chances are that many people in power, in both parties, are like Judas. They don't care about the poor, and they have their hands in the purse.

A more helpful perspective might be to view poverty as a disease. This idea includes the sense of systemic root causes such as circumstances, lack of opportunity and human mistakes. In any event, poverty diminishes all of us.

John Yoder, the Mennonite scholar, in his theological work *The Politics of Jesus*, claims that we misread the teaching of Jesus in many ways: We mistake the ethics of Jesus as simple rules for simple people, spiritual matters not social issues, individual ethics not government ethics, salvation ethics not social justice. Reductionism is a seriously flawed argument. We can see examples of reductionism in the news all the time.

Jerry Falwell Jr., a prominent Christian pastor, for example, makes the traditional case for fundamentalists when he says he is suspicious of churches that preach economic and social justice. This ignores, of course, Falwell's own social causes, such as anti-abortion. He wants the government to stay out of his business unless he needs the government to impose his social concerns on the rest of the nation. Witness his viral opposition to gay rights and gay marriage. By the way, his take on the issue of poverty is the opposite of the approach taken by the mainline churches and the Roman Catholic Church. From the social gospel of Washington Gladden, a famous Columbus, Ohio, Congregational pastor, to the long tenure of Dr. Charles Seasholes at First Baptist Church in Dayton, Ohio, there is a lasting opposition to American fundamentalism. Falwell's arguments have been around for almost two centuries and have changed little. His argument goes like this: Jesus wasn't interested in politics. Do you really think the Jewish leaders and the Roman Empire killed Jesus because he was a nice little rabbi who told stories and healed some people? Then Rev. Falwell says that those pastors who preach economic and social justice "are trying to twist the Gospel to say the Gospel supported socialism." The Gospel doesn't support socialism; that is a dehumanizing political philosophy that has failed miserably in our world. Falwell: "Jesus taught that we should give to the poor and support widows, but he never said that we should elect a government that would take money from our neighbor's hand and give it to the poor." Actually, Jesus taught that final judgment will be according to how well we cared for the poor. Read Matthew 25:2. Jesus says, "And the nations will be gathered before him." Nations, rulers, kings, presidents, elected officials, and governments will be judged. Finally Rev. Falwell says, "If we all did as Jesus did when he helped the poor, we wouldn't need the government."

Let's take a more critical look at this idea. In fiscal year 2000, federal, state, and local governments spent about $1 trillion on social welfare programs. How much money do American churches give? The Protestant churches in America give about $30 billion a year. If 10 percent is given to missions, that means that $3 billion was given to help others. If we gave the entire 3 billion dollars to aid the poor, it would equal three-tenths of 1 percent—yes .3 percent—of the amount of support now given by the government. Do we really think that the churches can eliminate poverty? This doesn't mean we shouldn't give. It means we should give more. But it also means that as Christians we should be grateful that some of our tax dollars help the least of our brothers and sisters. As Paul puts it in Romans 13: "Do what is good and you will receive God's approval. For the same reason you also pay taxes, for the authorities are the ministers of God. Pay all of them their dues, taxes to whom taxes are due, respect to whom respect is due, honor to whom honor is due."

Listen, the Bible and the teachings of Jesus are never just about individuals. God called Abraham, but he is never just an individual. He stands for all the promises of God to a people chosen by God. God chose a people and a nation. God chose Israel to be his servant and to be a blessing to all the nations of the world. And Jesus didn't just call a person to follow him. He called and commissioned a church—a body, a chosen race, a royal priesthood, a holy nation, God's own people.

What, then, should we do? How can we be faithful to the prophetic voices across the centuries that challenge us to care for the poor? St. Francis of Assisi, the Baptist theologian Walter Rauschenbusch, the Congregational pastor and theologian Washington Gladden, the Mennonite scholar John Yoder, the Catholic nun Mother Teresa. We can imitate the life of Jesus and the life of his saints.

Perhaps our attitudes need an adjustment. Do we resent poor people? Do we treat them as invisible? Do we respect the poor? William James said, "We have grown literally afraid to be poor. We despise anyone who elects to be poor in order to simplify and save his inner life. If he does not join the general scramble and pant with the moneymaking street, we deem him spiritless and lacking in ambition. We have lost the power even of imagining what the ancient idealization of poverty could have meant: the liberation from material attachments, the unbribed soul."

What if Mother Teresa had been the richest woman in the world? What if the people who are serving God in poor communities, teaching on Indian reservations, serving in the Peace Corps, and doing community organizing for the poor are the richest people in the world?

Yes, Jesus says, "The poor you always have with you." Well, what if that statement includes our own poverty because we are slaves to materialism and money, and we are diminished by a lack of trust, meaningful relationships, and healthy lives? What if Jesus meant this instead: "You will always be with the poor." Put that little word "with" in your mind for a moment. Roll it around in your heart. We are to be *with* the poor—with the poor always. Do we get it? Maybe not. An honest Christian said, "They make me nervous."

And here's the crucial teaching of the Gospel: Riches are found by being friends of the poor. If we refuse to make friendships with the poor, we will be impoverished. Will we take the risk of making new friendships in West Dayton and elsewhere?

Riches are to be found in being helpers of the poor: our intellect, our ingenuity, our experience, our leadership, our wealth, our understanding of the ways of power—everything we have. Lisa Delpit, in her book *Other People's Children*, says that the best thing we can do for poor children is to teach them the rules of success in our culture. With the status and power we possess in this community, we can help by speaking for and advocating for the poor. Before we break out into vicious arguments about how best to help the poor, we can take our stand and support the poor. There are more than 15,000 lobbyists in Washington, D.C., and precious few are there to advocate for the poor. Perhaps our own denomination needs to fund a professional lobbyist to speak for the interests of the poor. What if some of you used your financial and economic expertise to mentor a poor family by teaching them how to move out of poverty? Who among us will do the research to discover the transforming ideas and programs that are working and then teach us how to replicate those models?

Riches are to be found in discovering our role as priests. A priest is one who takes the gifts of the people and celebrates as God transforms the gifts of some into his blessings for all. If we are going to take seriously that we are a nation of priests, we are going to find ways to be priests to and for and among the poor. Then shall come to pass the saying of Jesus: "You will always be with the poor."

While that may not put us on the Forbes list of the richest persons in the world, it will put us on God's list of the faithful and richest people in the universe. What about it? Will you join me in being with the poor? As friends, helpers, and priests?

5

Does Jesus Save?

MARCH 28, 2010

Luke 19:28–40; John 12:12–16

A CHARACTER KNOWN AS the Misfit in a Flannery O'Connor story says, "If [Jesus] did what He said, then it's nothing for you to do but throw away everything and follow Him."[1]

Well, it's Palm Sunday, and everyone seems to be following Jesus. But appearances can be deceiving. Jesus refuses to play our games. My sermon is grounded in three theological claims:

- Jesus is to be understood in the historical framework of Judaism.
- His purpose is tied with the fate of the Jewish nation.
- His suffering and death are tied to the historical circumstances of the Gospel accounts. (Note: This is an inadequate summary of N. T. Wright's Third Quest for the Historical Jesus but will have to suffice.)[2]

This at least means that the Romans did not crucify Jesus because he could turn a nice aphorism or spin out archetypal metaphors or produce endless sound bites. After all, no one would crucify a popular preacher, a tenured professor, or a television "opinionator."

Let's accept the irony that while Jesus was innocent of the political charge, they did crucify him for the political reasons listed in the legal complaint. The title over his head says it all: "King of the Jews," written in three languages. And Pilate said, "What I have written, I have written." They crucified Jesus on the charge of treason. Jesus, our Jesus, was executed as a traitor.

One word defines the context of Jesus's life and death: Israel. The story of Jesus is the story of Israel retold with a new ending. Israel went to Egypt; Jesus went to Egypt. Israel comes up out of the land of Egypt; Joseph brings Mary and Jesus home from Egypt. Israel came to the Jordan River but lacked the faith to move forward; Jesus came to the Jordan, was baptized, and accepted the call of God to lead his people into the Promised Land. Israel was in the wilderness for forty years; Jesus was in the wilderness for forty days. Israel had twelve tribes; Jesus called twelve disciples. "Twelve" signifies Jesus's intention to remake the people of God.

Jesus bears all the hopes and promises of Israel. He is Israel: The second Adam, the one righteous man like Noah. He created a new people like Abraham and a new Israel like Jacob. Jesus liberated his people from slavery like Moses. Jesus was the ultimate king like David, the healer and troublemaker like Elijah, and a prophet like Jeremiah.

The kingdom of God is present where Jesus is. Where Jesus is, God is ruling the world. No wonder Paul shouts out, "Therefore God has bestowed on him the name which is above every name, that at the name of Jesus every knee should bow, in heaven and on earth and under the earth, and every tongue confess that Jesus Christ is Lord, to the glory of God the Father."[3]

Palm Sunday was the culmination of dreaming by people who had been following Jesus. At least one or more of Jesus's disciples were Zealots—the party of violence, national pride, patriotism, and zeal. They were tired of losing, tired of the Romans rubbing their noses in it. They were mad, and they were not going to take it anymore. Talk about hating the government. If there is any political emotion that we should understand, it is zeal. Red-faced zeal from every direction—left and right.

Hate groups are growing in America even as members of Congress and the media distance themselves from the on-the-ground results of their demagoguery. As even as the right demonizes President Obama, how quickly we forget the demonization of President Bush from the left. Americans have lost one of the three cardinal pillars of political rhetoric—ethos: credibility and respect. A Baptist preacher said: "'Render honor unto whom honor is due,' says St. Paul. These words throw a sacred guard around the administration and reputation of civil magistrates. The text enjoins a proper respect toward those who execute the law. They are not to be lowered and degraded in public esteem but are to be treated with candor and due respect, so that no man is at liberty to defame and revile them with impunity." The Baptist preacher who said that: the Rev. Doctor Thomas Armitage, of the Fifth Avenue Baptist Church in New York, on the last Sunday of May, 1880, as he "preached his last sermon prior to taking his summer leave of absence."[4]

American religion is Palm Sunday politics. We want Jesus as king, but we want to make Jesus kowtow to our prejudices. Jesus can't save us if we keep insisting that he be someone different.

We love the politics of Palm Sunday because we love parades and protests. At a parade, we can be happy; at a protest, we can be angry. They waved palm branches; we wave flags and guns, global warming papers, 2,000-page health care bills, and for some reason, the Constitution. Isn't there tragic irony in this picture of all sides of the political war dragging Jesus around like a rag doll, using Jesus like a dramatic prop, and piously intoning, "And may God bless America," in every political speech? Jesus isn't interested in the Second Amendment; he's interested in the greatest commandment—Love the Lord with all your heart, soul, and mind—and the second—Love your neighbor as yourself.[5]

Palm Sunday is high drama – like an oft-repeated Greek tragedy. I once interpreted this event as parody and heavy satire, but I have come to have less confidence in Jesus's so-called sense of humor. I believe this is serious drama and a serious visualization of all Jesus had been teaching. Or in more contemporary terms, Palm Sunday is Jesus's PowerPoint presentation: "I am not that kind of Messiah, but this kind." Jesus dresses for the starring role: Messiah—but not the crowd's idea of Messiah. Jesus acts out the prophecy of Zechariah: "Behold, your king comes to you triumphant and victorious, humble and riding on a donkey." You can feel the crowd's intensity, even without the hastily drawn signs we see today: "Here is Messiah. He has come to give us back our glory, our power, and our status." But the biblically literate crowd ignores the part of Zechariah's prophecy that it didn't like: that the king would be the Prince of Peace. The crowd sings, "Blessed is he who comes in the name of the Lord." These are words from Psalm 118, a "conqueror's psalm," thought to recall the great battle of 163 BC won by Judas Maccabeus. The crowd is too fired up to see what Jesus was saying: King of peace, not king of war. They don't get it. Jesus can't save us sitting under a palm tree.

There are two men, I believe (in an act of creative imagination), who were at the Palm Sunday parade, and they make a second appearance on the stage on Easter Sunday morning. They are oblivious to the resurrection and in despair: "We had hoped that he was the one to redeem Israel." I mention this because this is what happens to overzealous zeal, to putting all our hopes and dreams into one political party. But Jesus couldn't stop trying to help his people understand. So even as they dragged Jesus up the hill of Golgotha, he tried again to warn his people: "Daughters of Jerusalem, do not weep for me, but weep for yourselves and for your children. If they do this when the wood is green, what will happen when it is dry?" Jesus is like the green wood, and they are crucifying him. Men caught in blood lust can't hear the voice of reason, so Jesus appeals to the women: "Can't you see what is going to happen to your men who are like pieces of kindling?" Jesus can't save folks who see no need for being saved.

Now, let me outline the politics of the cross that are so different from the politics of Palm Sunday.

POLITICS OF PEACE

The politics of the cross are the politics of peace. Jesus came to town riding on a donkey. Did you know that the donkey was not a comic, ignorant, or even humble animal, but a noble beast in the ancient world? In peacetime, kings entered the city on a donkey. Only after victory in war did kings ride stallions into the city. Look at the statues in our capital city designed to enhance the heroism of the men they celebrate. They are astride magnificent semi-divine horses. It is no accident that Abraham Lincoln, the commander-in-chief who said, "With malice toward none and charity for all" – is sitting serenely[6]—"with malice toward none and charity for all."

POLITICS OF NONVIOLENCE

The politics of the cross are the politics of nonviolence. Jesus came to Jerusalem with a mission to bring about God's kingdom: "I am your king, but not on your terms." We can't control or manipulate Jesus. No resistance. No fighting back. No evil for evil. No getting even. No holding grudges or keeping score. Something is needed to break the cycle of our self-absorption and lack of mercy, and only a life— like that of Jesus, freely given with no hint of self-interest, can save us.

Jesus's opposition to violence covers everything in his teachings, and in order to practice our many forms of violence, we have to trample the teachings of Jesus. Our spiritual violence, the violence practiced in and by churches, perpetrated against other humans, includes anything that violates their humanity. Think of the church as a bull in a china closet, smashing the dignity and respect of human beings judged unworthy, wicked, sinful, and unwelcome. Jesus restores to membership in Israel those who had been on the margins of the holy society, whether through physical defects or through moral or social blemishes. How many unclean people does Jesus have to touch and heal before it sinks into our heads that the church is not to be a club designated only for the right kind of people? How many suffering women must he comfort and restore before we understand? How many thieves, publicans, sinners, lepers, prostitutes, adulterers, divorcees, gays, and lesbians must Jesus receive in mercy before it dawns on our thick hearts? How many outsiders must he bring inside? How many times must he eat with Matthew, Zacchaeus, and their assortment of friends? The church needs to get off its high horse and start riding that donkey.

POLITICS OF GOODNESS

The politics of the cross are the politics of goodness—the sheer goodness of God the Father. I believe Jesus does save, and what convinces me is how far Jesus was willing to go to make salvation possible. As Rowan Williams puts it, whatever needed doing, Jesus has done it. In the simple words of the Nicene Creed, "For us and for our salvation." In the memorable phrase from Eastern Orthodox liturgy, "You left nothing undone until you had brought us to heaven."

Some scholars, like John Calvin and the modern Roman Catholic Hans Urs von Balthasar, have said that Jesus on the cross is enduring hell itself. There's Scripture for the claim. In Ephesians 4:8–10, Paul says Jesus descended to the lowest parts of the earth "so that he might fill all things." And in I Peter 3:18–20, Jesus went and preached to the spirits in hell so they had a chance to hear the good news and be transformed by it. The point is that there is a way to salvation from any imaginable place. And in the Eastern Church, the resurrection of Jesus is pictured as Jesus breaking down the doors of a prison in which Adam and Eve, David and Solomon, and the Old Testament characters are bound. Somehow, Jesus "filled all things" and eliminated every dark place, every isolated desert, every wilderness, every black hole, and every valley of the shadow of death.[7]

Does Jesus save? Oh yes. As the psalmist says, from the highest heaven to the pits of hell, God is there. And wherever God resides, salvation is possible. From the uttermost parts of the sea? Oh yes! From the pits of hell? Even there. Jesus saves! Jesus saves!

ENDNOTES

1. Flannery O'Connor. "A Good Man Is Hard To Find."
2. See N. T. Wright. "Jesus, Israel, and the Cross." Wright makes eight points that are critical to the content of this sermon. 1. Jesus's ministry took its historical origin from that of John the Baptist, who warned Israel of the "wrath to come and urged her to return while there was still time. 2. This locates Jesus within Jewish apocalyptic expectation – the hope that God would soon, within the continuing course of history, act to vindicate his own name by delivering his covenant people from their current political and social predicaments. The referent is not to the end of the world but its purpose is rather to invest the future space-time events which are the actual referents with their true theological significance. 3. Jesus warned, not of the end of the world, but of the end of the present sociopolitical state of affairs. 4. What Jesus said and did challenged and disturbed the current expectations, the Jewish leaders, and the Roman Empire. Like Elijah, Jesus was a disturber of the status quo. The irony here is that we, Jesus's alleged followers, are often the keepers of the sacred status quo. 5. The primary category used by the followers of Jesus to explain Jesus was "prophet." 6. Within this developing picture, the numerous explicit warnings of the synoptic gospels fit comfortably. The action of Jesus in the temple was a symbolic act of destruction. 7. The warnings seem to have a concrete and historical referent: Rome will be God's means of bringing judgment on those who refuse to heed the warnings of Jesus. This is where Jesus turns on its head the Jewish expectation that God would act to save his people from Rome. For Jesus, hope lies, not in large-scale national deliverance from an enemy without, but in a national turning to a new form of aspiration. Caird and Borg both make the point that Jesus is saying, "If you persist in nationalist ambition, sooner or later Rome will crush you." 8. The so-called ethical teaching of Jesus is to be seen as the summons to Israel to be Israel—under Jesus's guidance. Here Borg offers a salient point: Jesus offers Israel an alternative paradigm, the "mercy code" of Luke 6:27–36 instead of the holiness code. Jesus calls us to be a welcoming, mercy-offering community, rather than an exclusivist company concerned with separation from defilement. This is a revolutionary Jesus of a different sort, but one who was making a definite political statement. Wright has 3 larger claims: Jesus warned Israel of the judgment to come; he identified himself with Israel; Jesus died because, as Israel's representative, he took upon himself the judgment which he pronounced against the nation. Carlyle Marney says that Jesus is the physician and when he looks the patient's chart, he discovers that he himself has the disease. I try to develop in this sermon the conclusion that Jesus died because of charges that amounted to sedition and treason: forbidding people to pay taxes to Caesar and claiming to be the King of the Jews.
3. Phil 2:9–11.
4. *New York Times,* 1880.
5. Matt 22:35–40.
6. William Sloane Coffin.
7. Rowan Williams, *Tokens of Trust.*

6

May God 'Easter' in Us

April 4, 2010

John 20:1–18

Welcome to Easter. Welcome back from the tautness of Lent, the tragedy of Good Friday, the terrifying wait in the darkness for this morning. Let me say at the outset: Easter is God's answer to death. So there was nothing in the religious experience of Mary Magdalene to prepare her for resurrection. Not in Greek paganism. Not in Judaism. Death, not resurrection, is humanity's commonplace.[1] Fleming Rutledge, an Episcopal priest and popular author, says she looks forward to Easter "more keenly each year as I get older, because there isn't anything we can do about death. It's so damned inexorable, and I do mean 'damned.' We feel its power as a hostile invading power." Dorothy Parker once said about death, "I do not approve." To the death angel we want to deny a passport, treat as terrorist. Death we know, but resurrection? That sort of thing doesn't happen around here.

Let us imagine "easter" as a verb.

- "Let him easter in us, be a dayspring to the dimness of us."[2]
- "Arise, shine; for your light has come, and the glory of the Lord has risen upon you."[3]
- "The sun of righteousness shall rise with healing in its wings."[4]
"Kings shall come to the brightness of your rising."[5]

God's "eastering" starts without us. By the time the first witnesses arrive, resurrection is accomplished. The second "Big Bang" is accomplished—a tumultuous surge of divine energy as fiery and intense as the creation. One author calls Easter "the fire in the equations," the energy in the mathematical and physical structures of things.[6] The stone is rolled away. Two angels, representing the mercy seat in the ark where God promised to meet his people, are in place. The linen cloths already neatly folded, a nice touch. God cleans up after death, sweeps it away in resurrection. God is always out in front of us. George Herbert's "Easter" puts it like this: "I got me flowers to straw thy way; / I got me boughs off many a tree: / But thou wast up by break of day, / And brought'st thy sweets along with thee."[7]

God's "eastering" in Mary Magdalene begins in darkness. "For behold, darkness shall cover the earth, and thick darkness the peoples." The residue of Good Friday is hard to shake. Death lingers: A year after the death of a loved one, a daughter still reaches for the phone to call her mother. Grief can shackle the spirit, rendering the mind dark, the heart shattered. Good Friday spreads its darkness even over Easter—over everything. Darkness covered the earth.

See "Mary weeping outside the tomb." Mary becomes the agent of memory and hope. Mary, one of a handful of witnesses to cross and resurrection, watched the man who had given her back her life die on the cross. "Without Jesus, Mary was empty." You can hear it in her words: "They have taken away my Lord." Part of Mary died with Jesus.

And then, there in the garden, Jesus stands. Alive again. Mary, blinded by grief, mistakes Jesus for the gardener. One of the most difficult themes of the resurrection is the depiction of Jesus as a stranger—mistaken for gardener, ghost, or fellow traveler. He compels us to be attentive to those of other races and cultures, of other faiths, of other Christian confessions. "To let the other be strange and yet not reject,"[8] to give and to be given attention—this is an essential part of Easter.

Look at Mary: Offered resurrection, she opts for busy work. "I will take away the body." A movie character hides from his grief by writing a bestseller on how to deal with grief and then travels the country as professional presenter around the universal theme of "I'm OK." But he wasn't. He was guilt-ridden, and staying busy wasn't working. Yet when God offers us actual transforming power of the Holy Spirit, we get busy and do religious stuff.

But then, the penultimate moment of Easter: "Mary! Mary!" Jesus calls her name. It's true isn't it? We long to be called by our name, known by God, and if known, loved. Resurrection makes God personal and invites us to live in friendship with God. God easters in life again. "Mary! Mary!"

Mary sees Jesus, as if for the first time, with new eyes. This is where resurrection impacts us the most. Believing in resurrection as a certain kind of doctrine can make Christians mean-spirited, but practicing resurrection is an "active condition of loving and nurturing, giving and forgiving, and seeing people in new, positive, and hopeful light."

When Jesus says to Mary, "Do not hold on to me," he summons her to a re-location of herself and a reinterpretation of her desire. As T. S. Eliot puts it, "What you thought you came for / Is only a shell."[9] Jesus grants Mary a whole identity again.

We can think about our beliefs as if they license us to impose them on all others, but such a spirit destroys the possibility of resurrection.

Perhaps some of you believe in resurrection as getting your life back again. Isn't that Mary's story? She had been a wreck, an emotional time bomb. And Jesus filled in the gaps and produced order in Mary's heart and mind. Have any of you raised a wayward son? Trouble at school? Mixed up in drugs? In court? On probation? And all the worry that your son was not going to make it? And then, somehow, a corner was turned, and like the waiting father in Luke's Gospel, you were able to say: "For this my son was dead, and is alive again."[10] If this is your understanding of resurrection, welcome to Easter.

Some of you may say, "I am a post-modern kind of believer. I don't think any of this happened in any literal fashion. Maybe you resonate with Marcus Borg's testimony: "I think the resurrection of Jesus really happened, but I have no idea whether it involves an empty tomb, and for me, that doesn't matter because the central meaning of the resurrection of Jesus is that His followers continue to experience Him as a living reality."[11] If this is your understanding of resurrection, welcome to Easter.

Some of you may say, "Jesus was raised bodily from the grave." Your faith resonates with John Updike's "Seven Stanzas at Easter" poem:

> Make no mistake: if He rose at all
> it was as His body;
> if the cells' dissolution did not reverse, the molecules
> reknit, the amino acids rekindle,
> the Church will fall. It was not as the flowers,
> each soft Spring recurrent;

> it was not as His Spirit in the mouths and fuddled
> eyes of the eleven apostles;
> it was as His Flesh: ours.
> Let us not mock God with metaphor,
> analogy, sidestepping transcendence;
> making of the event a parable, a sign painted in the
> faded credulity of earlier ages:
> let us walk through the door.

If this is your faith, welcome to Easter.

Let us be at peace with the simple affirmation of the ancient creeds: "On the third day he rose from the dead."[12] The question is whether we look even remotely resurrected. What needs to be happening around the church is that folks will show up, see what is here—credible, trustworthy people—and make the ultimate choice: "I want to live in the same world they live in; I want to know what they know and to drink from the same wells." Then others will be able to make the declaration: "I believe; I have confidence; I take refuge; I have come home." Unless God easters in us, there is no point in debating the resurrection. As God eastered in Mary Magdalene, a new hope, so God waits to easter in us.

Welcome to Easter!

ENDNOTES

1. The pagan world of Homer offers no resurrection. The cynical agnosticism of the first century is well expressed in funerary inscriptions: "I wasn't, I was, I am not, I don't care." In the Greek play *Eumenides*, Apollo declares that when a man has died, and his blood is spilt on the ground, there is no resurrection. First-century Judaism believed in a general resurrection at the end of time, but the resurrection of a person from the grave—the world of philosophy and religion simply says, "We know that kind of thing doesn't happen." The task of preaching on Easter Sunday intimidates a preacher. So as I read my way through a pile of academic papers and books about the resurrection and the postmodern world, the resurrection and science, the resurrection as mystical experience, the resurrection and Christian origins, life after death in Plato and the pagans, life after death in Judaism, the resurrection as a historical problem, proofs and historical verifications for the resurrection, the resurrection as story, narrative, edited church material [the things I do for you], an overwhelming conviction gripped my soul. My job as a pastor of a Christian church on Easter Sunday morning is to preach resurrection. See "Jesus's Resurrection and Christian Origins," "The Resurrection and the Postmodern Dilemma," "Can a Scientist Believe in the Resurrection?" by N. T. Wright; *Resurrection: Interpreting the Christian Gospel* by Rowan Williams; John Arnold's *Life Conquers Death*; David S. Cunningham, *Faithful Persuasion*; Reynolds Price, *A Serious Way of Wondering*.

2. Gerard Manley Hopkins, "The Wreck of the Deutschland." See also Nicholas Lash, Easter in Ordinary: "I do not know a better way of ending than with the conjunction of Herbert's "heaven in ordinarie" and Hopkins's use of "easter" as a verb. Living in relation, in the way that we do, to the unknown God, we do not possess, nor do we need to know, more of the form which the fullness of his eastering in all our ordinariness may take."

3. Isa 60:1–4 "Arise, shine; for your light has come, and the glory of the Lord has risen upon you. For behold, darkness shall cover the earth, and thick darkness the peoples; but the Lord will arise upon you, and his glory will be seen upon you. And nations shall come to your light, and kings to the brightness of your rising. Lift up your eyes round about, and see; they all gather together, they come to you; your sons shall come from far, and your daughters shall be carried in the arms. Then you shall see and be radiant, your heart shall thrill and rejoice."

4. Mal 4:2.

5. Isa 60:3b.

6. Kitty Ferguson, *The Fire in the Equations: Science, Religion and the Search for God*.

7. George Herbert, "Easter."

8. Rowan Williams, *Tokens of Trust*.

9. T. S. Eliot, "Little Gidding," quoted in *Tokens of Trust*.

10. Luke 15:24.

11. Marcus Borg and N. T. Wright have co-authored a book and debated one another for years. They are not on the same side concerning belief in the resurrection. Wright, a believer in the historical resurrection, has been criticized for saying that he believes Borg is a Christian.

12. The Apostles' Creed and the Nicene Creed ("on the third day he rose again according to the Scriptures").

7

If Seeing is Believing, Faith is Toast

April 11, 2010

John 20:19–31

For John, the interesting stuff happens on Sunday. On the Sunday after Easter, something really significant happened. A man who was dead appeared to the disciples alive, and Thomas was not there. We can take this from the perspective of a woman who once said, "I try never to miss church; I'm afraid something big will happen."

So on the next Sunday, Thomas is figuratively in church, and everyone is so glad to see him. He didn't just take his doubts and stay home. He came back to church the next Sunday. The other disciples start speaking in unison: "Thomas, you won't believe it. Jesus is alive, and he was here in church with us. He is risen from the dead, Thomas."

Thomas cries, "I will not believe it."

What if Thomas is not doubting intellectually but using his doubt as a protest against having to come to grips with this resurrected Jesus? There are all kinds of honest, anguished, emotional, yet intensely loyal doubt:

- The novelist Harry Crews: "I writhe and suffer in my unknowing. I don't know, and I want to know."

- William Faulkner: "The trouble with Christianity is that we haven't tried it yet."

- Dostoevsky: "It is not as a child that I believe in Christ and confess him. My hosanna has passed through a great crucible of doubt."

Make no mistake: We often go through doubt to discover faith. To accept that doubt keeps company with faith is not to celebrate doubt as a virtue but as reality. Garrison Keillor writes, " I came to church as a pagan this year, though wearing a Christian suit and white shirt, . . . a skeptic in the henhouse, thinking weaselish thoughts. This often happens around Easter. God sometimes schedules high holy days for a time when your faith is at low tide, and while everyone else is all joyful and shiny among the lilies and praising up a storm, there you are, snarfling and grumbling."

So doubt comes to church—not as lead soprano, but maybe a fourth-chair tenor, in the background (sorry, guys, but someone has to take one for the analogy here). Many churches don't know what to do with doubters. Novelist Lee Smith says, "I believe in God, but I can't find a church that doesn't put down or stamp out things I believe are basically good. It's something I struggle with all the time. Maybe I'll die struggling with it." You've heard of the mourners' bench. We have the doubters' bench, and it is wherever doubters sit waiting for the possibility of faith. The reason for being here is to walk together through the fire, the flood, the contradictions, and the possibilities.[1]

Then, of all things, Thomas demands special proof before he will believe in the resurrected Jesus. This is not a viable option for any of us. Seeing is not believing in our case. Believing has to be something much more substantial than seeing. Thomas sounds like a logical positivist or a scientist: "Show me the empirical evidence." You would think that Thomas had been schooled in truth theories: Correspondence, coherence, or Rorty's pragmatism. Well, Christianity has evidence, but not the scientific kind.

The church has an epistemological problem. We aren't sure how we know what we know. Epistemology is the study of human knowledge. And according to science, what we know, we know only on the basis of empirical evidence. If you can't see it, touch it, weigh it, measure it, it isn't true. But the church looks silly in lab coats, rattling around in a laboratory with test tubes, hypotheses, and theories, insisting she has proof that absolutely everything in the Bible is the literal truth. We do not operate in the world of proof and certainty, but in the world of faith and possibilities.

When Thomas says, "I will not believe," he has involved us in the world of rhetoric: opinions and beliefs.[2] In the opinion of Thomas, resurrection is an impossibility, so he discounts the testimony of his friends. True belief is trumped by mere opinion. Belief, in our age, often degenerates into dime-a-dozen opinions. When it comes to opinions, we often say, "My two cents' worth." In our world of big bucks, pennies and dimes are not exactly powerful. Yet in religion, opinion is the priesthood of the believer on steroids. Jesus doesn't seek opinion givers but faithful witnesses.

Thomas is more than a doubting disciple. He is an entire segment of the scientific community. As a leading evolutionary biologist, Richard Lewontin, put it, "We take the side of science . . . in spite of its failure to fulfill many of its extravagant promises of health and life because we have a prior commitment, a commitment to materialism. . . . for we cannot allow a Divine Foot in the door."[3]

So when Thomas says, "Unless I see the mark of the nails in his hands, and put my finger in the mark of the nails, and my hand in his side," he has involved us in the world of science—with all its empirical demands.[4] So science from the advent of the Enlightenment has proceeded to kick the church downstairs and take over the master suite. Empirical / empire / emperor. Get it? Maybe Galileo, harassed into recanting by an arrogant church, smiles in heaven at the rise of science, but I doubt it, because even under house arrest by papal authorities, Galileo was still a man of faith. Some Christians have groveled at the feet of science—worshiping it. Other Christians have violently opposed science, breaking out in hives at the mere sound of the name "Darwin" or the word "evolution." Still others have imitated the scientific method, to turn faith into a laundry list of fundamentals. By the way, creation, the ongoing processes of divine energy working in cooperation with humanity, doesn't belong in a museum. It's not dead.

Never doubt it. Science has made huge contributions to our well-being, but it must still bow in humility before the majesty of mystery. Science, for example, has been unable to account for how the billions of insentient neurons making up a human brain generate subjective awareness. It can't account for mental causation. If a scientist says, "Read my lips: No bodily behavior is produced by thoughts," the moving lips would be a performative contradiction. Christianity, more in tune with the poetic and the prophetic, concerns herself with the open windows of the mind and heart to see what might be possible in a world made by God. Science, like theology, has been humbled by the discovery that we know that we do not know. It turns out that Emperor Science wears rhetorical robes (Herb Simons, Toulmin, and Kuhn).

One word of caution: The attempt to approach human affairs as if they belonged to the world of evidence and determined outcome is bound to end in violence—ideological violence to the understanding of what humanity is and literal violence toward those who will not be convinced. The resurrection, in its narrative refusal of proof, is a statement of nonviolence, of radical patience with the unplanned and undetermined decisions of agents. Thomas Merton: "We believe that our future will be made in hope and love, not by violence or calculation."

Jesus enters the room where doubt has been so clearly expressed, the line drawn in the sand of intellectual debate, and says, "Peace be with you." He is gentle with Thomas. There's none of the insecurity, anger, and disdain for questioning that exists in his church these days. Jesus came and stood among his disciples and said, "Peace be with you." Then he said to Thomas, "Put your finger here, and see my hands; and put out your hand, and place it in my side; do not be faithless, but believing." There's no argument from Jesus. Isn't that refreshing?

Now listen to Thomas again. First, he said: "I will not believe." Now he cries, "My Lord and my God." Thomas moved from a desire for proof to personal relationship. Proof? If this is a fight over proof, the church isn't in the fight. We are poets, and we make possible new ways of being in relationship with God and the world.

Jesus, for his part, never offers proof; he just keeps passing out Easter invitations: Feed my sheep. Be my witnesses. Love one another. Make disciples. Baptize.

And when he was at table with them, he took bread, broke it, and blessed it, and they recognized him.

Thomas, no longer interested in proof, makes it clear what it means to affirm: "My Lord and my God." This Jesus, this raised-from-the-dead Jesus, his life, his death, his teachings, his examples, his commandments—this is what I accept as my way of being in the world. Thomas stands up to the crazed emperor Domitian, who insisted on being addressed as "Lord and God," and cries out, "Jesus is My Lord and my God." There is a saying in the Talmud: "You don't see things as they are; you see things as you are." To see things differently, one must be different. And this is the true story of Saint Thomas: courageous faith; not anguished doubt. The story you see has only one leading lady: Faith. "These things are written that you might believe!"

Let's not suppress any Thomas among us. Give him his head, like a good racehorse, and let him run with his doubt. But more than that, let's stick with Thomas because on the heels of his doubt, there's the possibility of a gigantic affirmation, a powerful confession of faith.

Meanwhile, save some seats in church for the doubters. There's the possibility of genuine faith embedded in the anguish of honest doubt. So if in the midst of the church's refrain of "Alleluia," your own faith is at low tide, and if while everyone else is "all joyful and shiny among the lilies and praising up a storm, there you are, snarfling and grumbling," there is so much hope for you. Don't dare let doubt keep you from Easter faith. Blessed are you, having not seen, and yet believing. Amen.

ENDNOTES

1. Thomas Merton.
2. The story of Thomas read through the lens of rhetoric and science offers an opportunity to consider the nature of belief, truth claims, and reality. For additional reading in the area of science as rhetoric, please see the following: Jacob Bronowski, *Science and Human Values*; Michael Polanyi, *The Study of Man*; John Ziman, *Public Knowledge: The Social Dimension of Science*; Thomas Kuhn, *The Structure of Scientific Revolutions*; Paul Newell Campbell, "The Persona of Scientific Discourse," *Quarterly Journal of Speech*, 61 (1975): 391–405; Herbert Simons, "The Rhetoric of Science and the Science of Rhetoric"; S. Toulmin, *The Philosophy of Science* and *The Uses of Argument*.
3. *New York Times*, Jan. 9, 1997.
4. Historically science and rhetoric have been antithetical disciplines. Science, we are told, deals with facts, certainty, and precision, which allegedly cannot be obtained with rhetorical methods. Rhetoric deals with contingent matters, while the aim of science is to empirically describe, explain, and predict events in the world. Rhetoric depends upon persuasion and an audience; science sets forth general truths without having an audience present. This sermon challenges this "received view." We are looking at rhetoric, science, and poetics as a framework for exegesis of a biblical text.

8

The Reliable God

April 25, 2010

Rev. 7:9–17, John 10:22–30

Our society suffers from mistrust and suspicion. Surfing the Web, I came across something called "liquid trust" and something called "the trust hormone." The natural ingredient produced in our bodies that increases our ability to trust is known as oxytocin. Scientists studying trust say that trust is absolutely central to a flourishing society. Without trust, societies fall apart. Add to this that periods of economic hardship produce tremendous stress. And guess what? Stress inhibits the release of oxytocin, the trust hormone. On a segment of NPR's All Things Considered, researcher Paul Zak, a neuroscientist and economist at Claremont Graduate University, suggested that mistrust during times of recession has a biological origin.[1] Think about this for a moment longer. There are people in America who are making their living encouraging people not to trust.

If trust is central to the network of relationships that constitute human society, then the church has a moral responsibility to speak for and on behalf of the power of trust. Trust is central. We need to be God's trust hormone in this untrusting world.

The problem goes to the very heart of our religious beliefs. Does God have credibility? Do we believe God is on our side? Plenty of people say no. It is open season on discriminating against God and destroying his reputation. God's civil rights are being denied, God's name smeared, God's character dragged through the mud. Have you heard of the Atheist

Bus Campaign in London? The ads were plastered on 800 buses: "There's Probably No God. Now Stop Worrying and Enjoy Your Life." Next, the American Humanist Association started a campaign in Washington, DC. "Why Believe in God?" over a picture of Santa Claus. "Just Be Good for Goodness Sake." I respond as a pastor who takes theology seriously to the mistrust that produces this kind of challenge to the credibility of God. As a member of the family, "I'm tired of it." Our faith in God is more than Freudian fantasy, figments of our imagination, or an infantile need for security. During the now-dead "God is dead" philosophy fad, a famous African-American preacher said, "God can't be dead. I'm a member of the immediate family and no one called me."

Borrowing a term from Aristotle, ethos,[2] which means character, credibility, or reputation, I want to demonstrate why we can trust God. Martin Heidegger says, "Ethos means abode, dwelling place." Revelation 5:11–14 shows God in his dwelling place, and all the multitudes and angels and elders and creatures falling before the throne in worship. The scene takes place in heaven, but its actual location is the real world of enemies and persecutors and suspicion and mistrust. God is not up in heaven basking in the glory of total credibility. God is here with us, patiently persuading us to move in the direction of heaven.

If God is going to have credibility, a powerful ethos, among us, *we must look at God's agenda.*[3] We can trust God because we can trust God's agenda. The world God made is designed to become a world at peace. No matter what our selfish, maniacal agendas, God has not one selfish purpose. God's agenda is rooted in complete generosity, an inexhaustible supply of love. "For God so loved the world." Wherever there is now violence, God intends peace. Where angry noise, praise.

The reading from Revelation shows a powerful scene of worship: the martyrs singing with all their hearts to the praise and glory of God almighty. The persecuted church of Jesus Christ, gathered in worship, sings in the face of the oppressive emperor of Rome. Sometimes only singing will bring us through the rough spots. Singing with passion and power can help us bear the burden. I'm tired, I'm weak, I'm lonely / Through the storm, through the night / Lead me on to the light / Take my hand, precious Lord, lead me home.

The Gospel group Sweet Honey in the Rock sings: I don't know how my mother walked her trouble down / I don't know how my father stood his ground / I don't know how my people survived slavery / I do remember, that's why I believe.

Now look at God's actions. We can trust God's actions. We can trust God precisely because he is the maker of heaven and earth. God is the source of everything—not part of the primeval matter of the universe, not an impersonal being in all animate and inanimate beings—but God almighty. This means we can trust the power of God not to be destructive, but positive. God employs God's power to overcome evil with good. In our world, absolute power corrupts absolutely. But with God, absolute power is absolutely trustworthy. God never asks, "What's in it for me?"

We can trust the presence of God—and make no mistake—presence is an action. Like a faithful shepherd—God shows the unlimited power to be there, to be faithful to and for a world that is deeply unstable and unjust and uncooperative: the power to go on trying to get through at all costs, laboring and wrestling with the human heart. If we leave home and family and friends for a new location, God is there. If we go through surgery, God is there. If we lose everything, God is there. Look at the number of places in Psalm 23: still waters, green pastures, the valley of death, right paths, table in presence of enemies. Place matters. "I have found my place." "I've been looking for this place my whole life." God keeps showing up to gently persuade us in the direction of what is best for us.

Jesus picks up the shepherd image from Psalm 23 and says, "I am the Good Shepherd. I am determined not to lose one of my sheep." No enemy will snatch them away. He is the Good Shepherd, and he lays down his life for his sheep. He will stand between his sheep and the enemies that threaten to destroy them: sin and death.

Now look at God's associations. Look at the associates of God: Father, Son, and Holy Spirit; angels and archangels; martyrs in white robes. And we stand in this line of apostolic succession. To us belongs the responsibility for enhancing the credibility of God.[4] Some people make up their mind about God by making up their minds about those of us who are associated with God. They have a rhetorically constructed set of ideas about the character of God, including the idea that God does not even exist. And God gains glory and blessing only as we demonstrate that the Lord our God is in the midst of us and that we are a peaceful, praising people.

I am not as interested in acts of intellectual prowess as I am in winning converts to the faith. We live in the "video-orality" age, and this demands a more active Christian community telling our story. Some of you think the best response to vicious and unwarranted attacks, to mindless theology, and to difficult social issues is to say nothing. You believe silence is golden. Well, in this cultural landscape, to say nothing is deadly. It did not please God to save the world by gathering groups of people to think deep thoughts. The measure of intellectual power is not how much we are able to theologically deny about God, but how much we are able to affirm; not how much we affirm human doctrines about God, but how much we persuade others of the glory of God. In other words, we should be more interested in rhetoric than dialectic.

"Dialectic seeks an act of the intellect"[5] such as, "I'll think about it."

Soren Kierkegaard said that the church requires more than information. At some point, dialogue about God demands a decision about God. Allow that something more to be an intelligent congregation, a rhetorically trained people, a Spirit-filled people who produce acts of persuasion, acts of the will, assent, and conversion. Thinking about God can be mentally invigorating, but actually speaking and living Christian lives with passion and integrity—that's our calling.

And in this way, God's reputation gains in stature and power. It may be the greatest need of the church in our day. Think of it: All of us working together to enhance God's credibility by completely trusting God in our daily lives. Aristotle said, "Character may almost be called the most effective means of persuasion he possesses." And since we are God's ambassadors, witnesses, orators, spokespersons, press agents, we must speak of the glory of God. We are God's "trust hormone" to the world.

Today let there be a vulnerable turning loose of everything to the trust of God. It is a time for making God credible by the intensity of our spirituality, the passion of our discipleship, and the depth of our commitment.

So here's the deal: Trust God and let go. Don't allow an atheistic scientist to erode your ability to trust in the goodness of God. It is not necessary to abandon the faith because an atheist somewhere in England yawned at the idea of God. Through it all, trust in God. Don't allow a tragedy to erase your faith in the power of God. The goodness of God is not compromised by the fact that we live in a risky world. Through it all, trust in God. Don't allow a difficult personal life to eradicate your belief in the trustworthiness of God. Through it all, trust in God.

ENDNOTES

1. NPR's All Things Considered, April 22, 2010.

2. Ethos (credibility), or ethical appeal, means convincing by the character of the author. We tend to believe people we respect. One of the central problems of argumentation is to project an impression that you are someone worth listening to, in other words making yourself into an authority on the subject, as well as someone who is likable and worthy of respect.

3. Ethos, according to Aristotle, originates in good will. I have changed this concept to consider God's agenda. God's agenda, aims, or goals are true indicators of God's good will. We exist because of the unconditional generosity of God. And God is determined to bring about a world of peace and praise. Please read once again Ephesians 1:3–14 for a renewed sense of God's agenda of peace and praise.

4. I have been discussing the ways God has credibility in our world as a result of God's agenda and actions. Now, I suggest rhetorically that we have a responsibility for the character of God in the world.

5. Marjorie O'Rourke Boyle. "A Likely Story: The Autobiographical as Epideictic." *Journal of the American Academy of Religion*, Vol. 57, No. 1 (Spring 1989), pp. 23–51.

9

When God Shocks Us

MAY 2, 2010

Acts 11:1–18; Revelation 21:1–6

START WITH A CHURCH fight. In the first-century church, some leaders attempt to stop Gentiles from becoming part of the church. Can you imagine such a thing as church leaders scurrying around the country, around denominational gatherings, gathering votes to keep folks out of church?

Meanwhile, back in Jerusalem, at church central, the church heard that the Gentiles had also accepted the word of God. I don't know when good news has ever received such a chilly reception. The Gospel is being preached. There should have been a celebration; instead, church members are angry. People from all walks of life are being saved. There should have been a celebration, but church members are ballistic. People are being baptized and filled with the Holy Spirit, but church members are complaining.

So what happens? Peter faces a church trial for converting a Gentile to the Gospel. Prosecutor's first question: "Why did you go to uncircumcised men and eat with them?" Table fellowship was a critical issue because it involved religious scruples. Leviticus 11, snatched from its historical context, becomes an easy target, but the rules in Leviticus were not intended to make God's people standoffish but to make them stand out as different, unique, and distinctive. It is about the food, but mostly, it's about faithfulness in a pagan environment. Most of us grew up with a long list of religious scruples. These scruples were part of the very fabric of our family and church lives, and they provided backbone and identity for our faith. Scruples really matter, and no doubt there is real pain on the part of these church members. These are not believers with oppositional defiance, but people standing up for what it meant to belong to God, and now Peter, in the name of Jesus and the Holy Spirit, is trampling on all this religious tradition.

I'm just saying that decisions about religious scruples and standards are not clear-cut. There's a world of difference between dropping a religious scruple just to go along with the world and dropping one under the direction of the Holy Spirit, the influence of prayer and study, and the command of God.

No wonder faithful Christians are determined to stop Gentiles from being part of the church. Imagine how these Christians feel after centuries of struggling to be the faithful people of God through oppression, wars, and exile; they were surrounded by a dark and pagan world, and now some upstart radicals want them to believe that God accepts Gentiles. People can get really angry when they think something is being taken from them or that something they love is being threatened. What if religious truth is not discontinuous but evolutionary?[1]

So Peter makes his defense, as Luke puts it, step by step. Some commentators on Acts claim that Peter doesn't argue; he just tells the story. Ambrose, an early church father, did once said, "It did not suit God to save his people by arguments."[2] Of course, that claim itself is an argument, and telling a story is also an argument. And the speeches in Acts are carefully constructed arguments by Luke as he makes the powerful case that "God doesn't show partiality, but in every nation anyone who fears him, and does what is right is acceptable to him."[3]

Meanwhile, back in Acts 10, Peter says, "I had a dream, and a sheet came down from heaven filled with all kinds of unclean animals and reptiles. God commanded me to eat unclean food. I refused the command." Several years ago, a preacher friend gave us a cookbook called *Critter Cuisine*. There are recipes for Dilly Quesadillos made from armadillo roast; batburgers; beak and claw surprise; tadpole consommé; and toad in the whole. Thinking of how disgusting that sounds, perhaps we understand Peter's revulsion.

How did Peter let go of his revulsion of Gentiles? Look at Peter on the rooftop of a seaside home overlooking the blue waters of the Mediterranean: warm breeze, seven-course meal, and fine wine. As he dreams, God reaches into the subterranean depths of Peter's unconscious mind, where there's a double-reinforced steel safe guarding all his deeply held religious scruples, and three times the dream is repeated.

I imagine that in the first version of the dream, Peter is shocked. God has a history of shocking us. God makes all things new, and we cling to all things traditional with white-knuckled fury. Isn't it odd that while God calls his people to go forward, the church has spasmodic movements in its history to go back?[4] But the book of Acts develops the story of Christianity spreading in a series of concentric circles, expanding "to the ends of the earth."

So God and Peter break into a full-blown argument. Don't be shocked. Hear Abraham arguing with God over how many righteous people it will take to save a wicked city.[5] Hear Moses arguing with God over not destroying a stiff-necked and disobedient people.[6] Hear Job arguing with God over suffering and righteousness.

The second time, I can imagine God saying, "I hear you Peter, but let me remind you that I sent Jonah to preach repentance to the great city of Nineveh—a place full of Gentiles. I have made of one blood all nations of the world." A flummoxed Peter pulls out old arguments for his scruples and runs all his favorite proof texts up the flagpole of tradition. No doubt, he quoted Leviticus 11. After all, Christians under fire often resort to quoting Leviticus. Every species of living being that was on the menu for Peter, wrapped in that sheet, was expressly forbidden as food in Leviticus.

The third time, my guess is that an agonizing Peter finally lifted himself out of the stew of his religious scruples and started listening to the message of God. A blind person can memorize all the furniture in a room and become comfortable moving around in the darkness. This can also happen to people who can physically see but are spiritually blind. They simply get used to the darkness and move around comfortably as if light has shone from on high. Remember the words of Jesus to the Pharisees: "Blind guides, straining out a gnat and swallowing a camel." Sweet irony, since the camel is one of the animals that the Jews are specifically prohibited from eating in Leviticus 11. Jesus says, in effect, "You would never eat a camel steak, but here you are swallowing a camel by ignoring 'justice and mercy and faith.'"

And maybe, just maybe, during the third lesson, Peter realizes his surroundings. Sometimes the message is the scene. Peter is at the seaside house of Simon the tanner—permanently unclean because he works with dead animals. First ray of light: Stay in the home of someone who has been excluded. Get to know them. Have dinner with them. If you go back and read Acts 10, you will discover that Peter finally did as God told him to do. He goes to see Cornelius, and he says, "You common, ordinary man, I don't like it, but God sent me here." Peter's still talking like a person in first class is better than the folks in coach. This may be one of the worst sermons in Christian history, but God uses it to convert Cornelius. "Behold, I make all things new."[7]

Then, of all things, the church says: "Then God has given *even* to the Gentiles the repentance that leads to life." Before we break out singing "Victory in Jesus," the church still can't quite accept the new reality: "*Even* those people." The church will flip-flop.[8] Scholars of the philosophy of science argue whether scientific knowledge is revolutionary and discontinuous or evolutionary and cumulative.[9] I believe that religious truth, at times, is evolutionary and builds on earlier ideas. Breaking through is hard to do.

So behind the story of Peter was what God had been trying to say all along: Abraham's call to be a blessing to all the nations; Solomon's prayer that the Temple be a place of prayer for all peoples; Jonah's preaching mission to Nineveh; Jesus's sermon that included the Zarephath widow and the Syrian general. So, when the first church conference convenes in Jerusalem, this is not a discontinuous event. This is an event built upon a message always embedded in the heart of God.[10] From the get-go, God elected to save all.

So if you dare to do it, take the most important religious scruple you have, and do some Bible reading. Read, "What God has cleansed, you must not call unclean." Read, "Truly, I perceive that God shows no partiality, but in every nation any one who fears him and does what is right is acceptable to him." Now, read Romans 14: "Do not, for the sake of religious scruples, destroy the work of God."

Describe to God in minute detail your hangups about certain groups; make it sound as mean-spirited as it actually is in your heart. List every stereotype you have ever heard about the group you despise. Read the Scripture and tell God how you really feel about Muslims or Democrats or gays or Catholics or African-Americans or Tea Partiers or skinny people or rich people. Do it three times. You will get bored with your own angry bitterness. Then on the third time, just maybe, something new: the white-hot light of God's grace will dawn on your cold anger, and you will exchange an inadequate belief for the grace of a God who accepts anyone in any nation who fears God and does what is right and makes all things new.

ENDNOTES

1. This is the key question in this sermon, and the answer comes later in the discussion about whether or not change is revolutionary or evolutionary. The analogy borrows from a debate in the philosophy of debate between Thomas Kuhn and Seven Toulmin.

2. "For they store up all the strength of their poisons in dialetical disputation, which by the judgment of philosophers is defined as having no power to establish anything, and aiming only at destruction. But it was not by dialectic that it pleased God to save His people; for the kingdom of God consists in simplicity of faith, not in wordy contention" (Ambrose, *De Fide*, I:42).

3. This is a crucial issue for the church, so Luke tells the story twice—once as a historical narrative in Acts 10 and again in Acts 11 as a narrative explanation or witness or testimony by Simon Peter. See Jaroslav Pelikan, *Acts*, *Brazos Theological Commentary on the Bible*; Johannes Munch, *The Acts of the Apostles*, *The Anchor Bible*, 31.

4. Nineteenth-century restorationists such as Alexander Campbell tried to restore in his time what he considered the pristine New Testament church. An article in *The Christian Science Monitor* surveys a group known as the "New Puritans"—Christians bringing back the austere doctrines of John Calvin. The popular way of expressing this form of Calvinism is TULIP: Total depravity, Unconditional election, Limited atonement, Irresistible grace, and Perseverance of the saints. The most difficult of these beliefs: predestination, called by a leading Greek Orthodox scholar, "the most heretical idea in Christian history" (David Bentley Hart).

5. Gen 18: Remember how Abraham argued with God over how many good people it would take to keep God from destroying Sodom? "Lord, surely there must be some good people in Sodom." And the "judge of the earth" must be fair to them; you can't just destroy the good with the bad. And God allows Abraham to do this bargaining and haggling. Abraham puts his whole heart into getting God to reduce the number of good people there needs to be in the city for God to spare it. The story is telling us that God can be trusted to do right. Whenever I am tempted to agree with the doomsday prophets that our country is finished, that our city is hopelessly lost, I like to read this story of Abraham arguing with God. There is great comfort in the idea that it only takes ten good people to keep a city alive. Remember how Moses argues with God after the associate pastor, Aaron, had been persuaded to make a golden calf. God's anger is aroused at the behavior of Israel and vows to destroy the entire mob. And Moses says: "You can't do that; you have promised to be faithful to this people. Do you want the rest of the world to say that you ran out of patience, that you couldn't cope with them after all, that you couldn't keep your promises?" Moses is pleading, begging, cajoling God. A little later in the story, Moses goes even further: "If you won't forgive them, don't make an exception of me: blot my name out of your book as well." Imagine Moses saying, "I don't want to be involved with a God who changes his mind and isn't capable of forgiving and starting again with the same old sinful and stupid people. What matters to Moses isn't his own safety or future; what matters to him is that God is still trustworthy

because he sticks with his people and refuses to tear up his promises.

6. Rowan Williams, *Tokens of Trust*.

7. Rev 21:1–6. See J. Massynberde Ford, *Revelation, The Anchor Bible*, 38.

8. Peter has ongoing issues with the issue of allowing Gentiles into the church. In Gal 2, Paul tells us, "But when Peter came to Antioch I opposed him to his face, because he stood condemned. For before certain men came from James, he ate with the Gentiles; but when they came he drew back and separated himself, fearing the circumcision party. And with him the rest of the Jews acted insincerely, so that even Barnabas was carried away by their insincerity." Acts 15, Gal 2, and Acts 21 are crucial texts for grasping what a controversial issue the inclusion of Gentiles really was for the early church. This was not a foregone conclusion. Christianity could have ended up as a small sect of Judaism and not as a worldwide religion.

9. Thomas Kuhn, *The Structures of Scientific Revolutions,* and Steven Toulmin, *The Uses of Argument*.

10. For some reason, it seems Paul left the conference before James announced the compromise resolution. While Acts 15 seems to indicate this was a decision made by James alone, I believe James is reporting the consensus of the church and not indicating that he was the sole authority for the church. In any event, Acts 21 says that Paul finds out only later about the compromise agreement over Gentile inclusion. There are numerous places in the New Testament where the issue appears. See Acts 21:17–26. The Nazarite vow about shaving the head comes from Num 6:1–21. In Acts 16:3 Paul took Timothy and circumcised him because Paul's opponents were spreading the rumor that Paul was teaching all the Jews to forsake Moses, telling them not to circumcise their children or to observe the customs. This was not true, but it shows how nasty this sort of thing can get in church. For Paul, this represents compromise; for Timothy, it was a bloody, painful sacrifice. In 1 Cor 9:20, Paul says, "To the Jews, I became as a Jew; to those under the law I became as one under the law."

10

A Woman's Place

MAY 9, 2010

Acts 6:9–15

ABIGAIL ADAMS, WRITING TO John, her husband: "In the new code of laws which you make, I desire you would remember the ladies, and be more favorable to them than your ancestors. Do not put such unlimited power into the hands of their husbands. 'Remember all men would be tyrants if they could' [line of poetry from Daniel Defoe]."[1]

Lydia is the lady we remember on this Mothers' Day—a single mom operating a business. Luke tells us she was a dealer in purple cloth. Let us consider Lydia in the context of Mothers' Day and a woman's place.[2]

See Lydia's place as a booth in the affluent marketplace of Philippi. Purple cloth was the Gucci handbag of Roman times. And Lydia sells purple cloth and purple robes. Purple stands in the ancient world for everything that matters in our world: Money and power.

Lydia: successful entrepreneur and businesswoman. It takes a sassy and powerful woman to succeed in a world that stacks the odds against her. My favorite sassy television character was Julia Sugarbaker. In an episode of *Designing Women*, Julia gives a photographer a piece of her mind when he wants her to straddle a stool and put a pearl necklace in her mouth for a magazine feature on successful Atlanta businesswomen. Stereotypes die hard, and sassy women devour them for breakfast. Julia says: "I'm saying I want you and your equipment out of here now. If you are looking for somebody to suck pearls, then I suggest you try finding yourself an oyster. Because I am not a woman who does that, as a matter of fact, I don't know any woman who does that, because it's stupid. And it doesn't have any more to do with decorating than having cleavage and looking sexy has to do with working in a bank. These are not pictures about the women of Atlanta. These are about just the same thing they're always about. When you start snapping photos of serious, successful businessmen like Donald Trump and Lee Iacocca in unzipped jumpsuits with wet lips, straddling chairs, then we'll talk."

Purple also had serious religious meaning. Purple appears in many places in the Bible. Maybe purple was God's favorite color. In Exodus, we discover that the garments of the priesthood and the curtains separating the holy of holies from the rest of the tabernacle were made of purple, blue, and scarlet. So purple is no ordinary color.

See Lydia's place on the Sabbath: down at the riverside at a prayer meeting with other women. Imagine Lydia not at the market—the ancient equivalent of the New York stock exchange—but on the Sabbath, drawn with other women to the river for prayer, to share burdens, to re-create. A woman's sadness can drive her to prayer: Sweet Honey in the Rock, a singing group of African-American women, sings: "Sometimes I feel like a motherless child, a long, long way from home. Sometimes I feel like I'm almost gone, but I hear my mother calling me, come on home child."[3] *The Color Purple*, by Alice Walker, is a prayer book (what else would you call a book full of letters to God) by a woman who learns, in the face of abuse and suffering and mistreatment, how to laugh, to play, and to love. As Lydia and the sisterhood of prayer meet at the river, there are no men in the gathering. No rabbi for the preaching. What will the women do? When God's people have no clergy, they do what God's people have always done: They "clergy" on. God's people have always been able to preach the word, teach, baptize, and have church with or without benefit of clergy.

To this gathering of strong, independent, God-fearing women comes the message of the Gospel. And the response of Lydia to the good news: "The Lord opened her heart to listen eagerly to what was said by Paul." Please think of eagerness as a divine possibility and a gift of grace. Only an open heart can produce eager faithfulness.[4] It is powerful thing when a woman says, "I have given you my heart."

Get the purple robe for Lydia and all our mothers and clothe them in royalty and priesthood. Any woman who has raised a husband and hard-headed, attention-defying children is already a priest and deserves a PhD. After all, a mom hears fears, dreams, and confessions, and she takes within her heart the pain and suffering of her children. The old joke is that PhD stands for "piled higher and deeper," so get deep blue chevrons for that robe, and put a purple stole around her neck, because like laundry on a Saturday morning, life often piles in higher and deeper. Remember these beautiful, compassionate priests, draped in God's color,[5] royalty's color, the priestly color.

Lydia stands in the long line of women who have opened their hearts to God. Remember the ladies. Remember Phoebe, a deacon in the church.[6] Remember Monica, mother of St. Augustine.[7] Remember St. Julian of Norwich,[8] who in the fourteenth century said, "Our Savior is our true Mother in whom we are endlessly born and out of whom we shall never come." By the way, Julian's work, *Revelations of Divine Love*, was the first book by a woman ever published in English. There's a host of women who marked the way for the "brightest and best" Christian women who now serve in pulpits across America.[9]

Remember the ladies. Every man preaching in a Baptist church was taught the Bible and received his basic theological training from a woman Sunday School teacher. At what point does a woman's wisdom become inadequate for the church? A woman taught us to name the books of the Bible in Vacation Bible School—a weeklong veritable stuffing of children with Bible verses, songs of faith—"Deep and wide, deep and wide, there's a fountain flowing deep and wide"—and saltine crackers and Kool-Aid. (The Baptist city kids got RC Cola and pecan sandies.)

A woman taught us how to pray, to read our Bibles, to love our neighbors, and to love Jesus. How long are Christians going to tolerate the patently absurd and pagan notion that a woman should not be a priest or a pastor? After all, first-century attitudes toward women were degrading, and now they have the sanction of the Roman Catholic and Southern Baptist churches. It's still paganism, no matter how many Bible verses they quote.

See Lydia's place as her home in Philippi. Lydia and her household are baptized, and she urged us, saying, "If you have judged me to be faithful to the Lord, come and stay at my home." And she prevailed upon us. And Luke tells us the church gathered in Lydia's home.[10]

An open heart and an open home equal Christian hospitality. Perhaps it is true that a home means more to a woman than it does to a man. Lydia makes a radical response to the Gospel. Her business is jeopardized because her clientele are the very people who had Paul and Silas arrested. She risks everything for her newfound faith.

So, where is a woman's place? Yes, I have deliberately used a phrase that is commonplace among those who piously intone, "A woman's place is in the home taking care of her children and her husband." Well, I turn that phrase on its prejudiced, abusive, and ugly little head. Did you say, "A woman's place?" A woman's place is wherever she chooses, wherever she gives her heart, velcroes her resilient spirit to the wall, and puts to work her intelligent, creative, and nurturing power. A woman's place is where she finds fulfillment, purpose, and joy. A woman's place is wherever she makes it, wherever God guides her and opens doors for her. A woman's place may be in the White House or her own home, as CEO of a corporation or CEO of three kids. The Catholic Church could use a woman pope, and as Will Campbell says in his satirical novel, *The Convention*, the SBC needs a woman president.

When a woman makes a place, it really is a place. It is a place of honor and dignity, a place for others because of its unselfishness, a place for growth and warmth. A woman may be the best maker of place in the world, often against overwhelming and abusive odds and with huge male opposition.

Look around this sanctuary at the wonderful mothers who are also successful lawyers, professors, corporate managers, teachers, accountants, homemakers, CEOs, office administrators, real estate agents, and a host of other vocations. Take a moment and remember the ladies. Remember our moms, those living today and those who have gone to a place not made with hands—a place reserved in heaven, a place created not just by God the Father, not just by the act of Jesus Christ the Son, but also by the creative, nurturing, feminine Holy Spirit. And that, my friends, is a woman's place. And it is our best chance for heaven on earth. *Vi-ve le vin, vi-ve l'a-mour, vi-vent les filles a la nuit comme le jour!*[11]

ENDNOTES

1. David McCullough, *John Adams*, p. 104. The rest of the letter from Abigail: "If particular care and attention is not paid to the ladies we are determined to foment a rebellion, and will not hold ourselves bound by any laws in which we have no voice or representation. That your sex are naturally tyrannical is a truth so thoroughly established as to admit of no dispute, but such of yours as wish to be happy willingly give up the harsh title of master for the more tender and endearing one of friend. Why then not put it out of the power of the vicious and the lawless to use us with cruelty and indignity with impunity."

2. I am aware that the title of this sermon, "A Woman's Place" has a rhetorical history that suggests that an woman's place is a narrowly proscribed and dictated place. A woman's place is vigorously defended by Fundamentalists, Southern Baptists, and Roman Catholics, among others. These groups do this even as they depend upon the work of women to sustain their institutions. Fundamentalists, in particular, are irritating when they insist on sticking their religious noses into the affairs of families. They need to learn how to MYOB. In any event, the strategy of this sermon is to turn the phrase "A woman's place" into a different set of meanings—meanings that have more width, more depth, and more generosity of spirit.

3. Sweet Honey in the Rock.

4. A James Autry poem about his grandfather preacher came to mind here as I discussed eagerness: "O God let him go dreaming when he goes let him go preaching a revival meeting with the congregation eager beyond discomfort." James Autry, *Nights Under a Tin Roof.*

5. God wants to be loved. Quote from *The Color Purple*, Alice Walker: "Listen, God love everything you love—and a mess of stuff you don't. But more than anything else, God love admiration." "You saying God vain," I ast. "Naw, she say. Not vain, just wanting to share a good thing. I think it pisses God off if you walk by the color purple in a field somewhere and don't notice it. . . . Everything want to be loved. Us sing and dance, make faces and give flower bouquets, trying to be loved. You ever notice that trees do everything to git attention we do, except walk?" (pp. 178–179).

6. Rom 16:1 ff.—"I commend to you our sister Phoebe, a deacon of the church at Cenchreae, for she has been a benefactor of many and myself as well. Greet Priscilla and Aquila, the preachers, who work with me in Christ Jesus, and who risked their necks for my life, to whom not only I give thanks, but also all the churches of the Gentiles. Greet Mary who has worked very hard among you. Greet Andronicus and Junia, my relatives, who were in prison with me; they are prominent among the apostles, and they were in Christ before I was. Greet those workers in the Lord, Tryphaena and Tryphosa (twins)."

7. In the calendar of Saints, Monica, mother of St. Augustine, is honored May 4.

8. Julian's day in the Calendar of Saints is May 8.

9. There's a baptismal affirmation, from the first century of the church's life, recorded for posterity in 1 Pet and spoken over the newly baptized as they came dripping from the pool: "You are a chosen race, a royal priesthood, a holy nation, God's own people in order that you may proclaim the mighty acts of him who called you out of darkness into his marvelous light. Once you were not a people, but now you are God's people; once you had not received mercy, but now you have received mercy." The church has never baptized only the men. And in that baptism and in that promise, ordination has already been accomplished. The rest, all that clerical power grab by men, is window dressing.

10. When Paul and Silas got out of the Philippi jail, "they went to Lydia's home; and when they had seen and encouraged the brothers and sisters there, they departed." The brothers and sisters suggest that the church in Philippi met in the home of Lydia.

11. Cajun group Bonsoir catin, Lafayette, Louisiana.

11

Understanding Others

May 23, 2010

Acts 16:16–34; John 17:20–16

Pentecost means that God has formed a new people: a church. He's given us a mission to form a universal fellowship. Pentecost is the reversal of the Old Testament story of the Tower of Babel's confused tongues. Pentecost is all the understanding in the world for all the people in the world. In a world of misunderstanding—politics, economics, environment, ethics, theology, religion, culture—what could matter more than understanding? As I. A. Richards, the philosophical godfather of the conservative political movement in America, puts it: Rhetoric is the study of misunderstandings and their remedies. And so is the experience of Pentecost. Think of it: the remediation of misunderstanding—work of the church.

God said, "I will pour out my Spirit upon all flesh."[1] It's an unlimited resource of spiritual power, and we are the containers. It's the new wine of God poured from heaven's vats, and we are the wine jugs of the new age. So Pentecost claims that we have all the assets necessary to produce understanding.

Nothing fosters understanding like giving. Do we see that God has always been in a giving relationship with all flesh? Pentecost was the spiritual equivalent of Christmas morning. Under the tree of life, we have a pile of gifts, as if out-of-control grandparents were in charge of the giving. As Paul puts it in Ephesians 4: "He gave gifts to his people." The writer of Hebrews insists that in Jesus Christ the entire universe coheres. "It should be a rather exhilarating thought that the moment of creation is now." God's giving; the outpouring of God's energy is now. This amazing world and what we were designed to be is sheer gift.[2] So Pentecost fulfills the prophecy that those with lips that could not speak, those with eyes that could not see, those with ears that could not hear, those with hearts that were cold, those with minds that could not understand would now prophesy, dream, and see visions. Pentecost is *now*.

God has poured his powerful, life-creating love into the world, but we are suspicious. The philosophers of suspicion have hammered away at the faith and lured us into theological accommodations. We have gone overboard in embracing the questions and objections to our strange faith that Jesus is the savior of the world.[3] What about all those people who never had a chance to hear about Jesus? What about all the generations before Jesus? Doesn't this claim give the church the perfect excuse for trying to shut up anyone who is not Christian? Isn't that the attitude that gave us crusades, inquisitions, holy wars, witch hunts, colonialism, empires, and genocide? How can the truth of Jesus, spoken 2,000 years ago, be truth for today? How can there be one truth in a plural world? Let's face it: These are serious moral, political, and philosophical objections.

Some Christians think that preaching Jesus as savior of the world makes you an intolerant bigot toward those with other convictions. In a plural society, eternal truth is suspect. Church members are content to practice faith silently in a *public* that values plurality over truth. We fail to notice that some pluralism is the doctrine of free will in a highly degraded form—the form of choices, options, and everything goes. The only ethical criteria: Is it fun? Do I like it? Am I comfortable? But this is a distorted pluralism.

The pluralism of the Pentecost crowd was not intended to create a world of individuals each doing his or her thing. After all, we have a plurality of religious convictions, lifestyles, philosophies, and options. And a lot of churches have opted to embrace this easy-going world of options because it is more comfortable, less taxing, and not so embarrassing as going around the world proclaiming a universal Gospel with a universal truth. We are careful not to appear as overly invested in matters of faith. Erving Goffman, in *The Presentation of Self in Everyday Life*, points out that all participants in social interactions are engaged in certain practices to avoid being embarrassed, and this seems to happen to Christians who are not willing to bear witness to their faith.[4]

Yet on Pentecost, God unleashes the Holy Spirit to empower a people to proclaim the message of Jesus Christ to the whole world. No doubt a bewildered church has turned Pentecost into a party with cake and candles, but it is really wind and fire. Instead of singing "Happy Birthday" to us, we are supposed to be saying, "Let me tell you about Jesus."

Should we simply abandon the idea of eternal truth? Of course not. If the price we pay for interfaith dialogue is to give up our truth claim about Jesus, the price is too high. If the price we pay for friendship with the world is to deny the uniqueness and finality of Jesus, the price is too high. If the price we pay for an alliance with science, so that we are allowed to touch the hem of the lab coat, is to give up our truth claims about the goodness and power of almighty God, then the price is too high. Doesn't that put us with Peter in the garden of Pilate? "I don't know him."

The church created on Pentecost is meant to be the affirmation of Jesus, not the denial. "There is now on earth a community which proclaims God's will for universal reconciliation and God's presence leading us towards full humanity."[5] And how those who don't accept Jesus are related to God, we just don't know. "What happens to those who never heard of Jesus?" turns out to be a question demeaning the character of God. Paul says, "Ever since the creation of the world [God's] eternal power and divine nature have been seen through the things [God] has made." The psalmist, who had a more spiritual connection to creation than many Americans who despise environmental concerns, says the sun and moon praise God along with the shining stars, fire and hail, stormy wind, and mountains.[6] Our role is to share, not to argue about what God is going to do about those who have never heard. We shouldn't doubt God's communication skills.

Pentecost offers largeness of spirit, generosity, compassion, and community. "It seems to me that in joining the church, you join a larger, full-color world. The whole world is your new neighborhood, and all who dwell therein—black, white, yellow, red, stuffed and starving, mighty and lowly . . . all become your sisters and brothers in a new family formed in Jesus. By joining the church, you affirm community on the widest possible scale."[7]

The church is this amazing kaleidoscopic community of universal giftedness, this cornucopia of mutual understanding. This is what makes whining such an offense to God. It is the same idolatry of the Israelites whining in the wilderness because God fed them manna when they wanted meat. No wonder so many church folk have a restaurant mentality and think church provides a menu for their demanding tastes. There's something tragic about the scene of a pastor bouncing out on a stage and saying to the congregation, "Let me tell you about our specials today."

Have you ever noticed that there are churches that operate under a herd mentality, a kind of *Stepford Wives* sameness? It is not too much of a stretch to use Goffman's term "total institution" for such churches. He was describing prisons and mental institutions, but listen closely to his definition: "All aspects of life are conducted in the same place and under the same single authority. Activities are always in the company of large batches of similar others, where there are explicit rules, and a body of officials all according to a single overall plan." Church was never meant to be a confining prison but a releasing of freedom and gifts of all. Church is meant to look like the Pentecost crowd: multinational, multicolored, multitribal.

As we experience the poured-out gift of the Holy Spirit, we have enlarged capacity to understand others. Two very different kinds of beings come to know one another in the movie *Avatar* and say, "I see you." I see in your heart. I see how much we are alike. I love you. It's the South African concept of Ubuntu: I see you. When we "see" persons of other religions, we will learn. Something in their humanity and their faith will challenge and enlarge ours but not compromise it. We will emerge from our relationships with others and say that we have learned something we never dreamed of, and our discipleship will have been enriched in gratitude and respect.

This understanding is a critical part of the Pentecost experience: Each could hear in his and her own native tongue. No one exists in isolation or grows up in isolation or suffers in isolation. This is part of what happens when we are willing to be with people different from us. We learn to see what the other person's face looks like when it is turned to God. And we have no right to go beyond this point because the sign in the road says, "Beyond this point—God only." Many Christians can't resist claiming there is no hope for those outside the family of faith, and Christians have even been known to say there is no hope for those outside their particular brand of faith. It is so hard for us to not meddle in classified folders stamped "For God's eyes only." Let God be the judge of how anyone outside the Christian faith is related to Jesus. There are lives of people who are not Christians—Jews, Muslims, Buddhists, agnostics—that are characterized by principles and values central to the Gospel. There are lives that are so obviously bathed in Christlikeness, so baptized in the meekness, humility, gentleness, and love of Jesus that it would be foolish for any of us to say it has nothing to do with the act of God through the Son and the Spirit. I am content to let God decide what is going on in the lives of such faithful ones.

This, then, is Pentecost: an overwhelming desire to share with others because God has poured out her Spirit on all flesh; the humble desire to learn from others different from us (each in his own native tongue); and the patience and good sense to let God work out her purpose for all humanity as is best in her eyes. O Lord, grant us wisdom, grant us courage that we might be the church of Pentecost.

ENDNOTES

1. When Peter is accused of being drunk, I thought of the image of PUI—preaching under the influence—of the Holy Spirit. This is the church's calling, and this is to be the intensity and regularity of our Christian witness. There are two basic conclusions that follow in the sermon: It is unfair to say that we don't have to share; and it is unfair to say that there is no access for some.

2. Rowan Williams, *Tokens of Trust*. It was Rowan Williams week in my study. "It should be a rather exhilarating thought that the moment of creation is now—that if, by some unthinkable accident, God's attention slipped, we wouldn't be here. It means that each of us is already in a relationship with God before we've ever thought about it. It means that every object or person we encounter is in a relationship with God before they're in a relationship of any kind with us. And if that doesn't make us approach the world and other people with reverence and amazement, I don't know what will."

3. Rowan Williams, "The finality of Christ in a pluralist world," a lecture during a visit to the Diocese of Guildford, March 2, 2010. I depended on this lecture for two major paragraphs in the sermon because I found it to be a concise argument for how we can maintain our commitment to Jesus as savior of the world in a pluralist culture and maintain our integrity without compromise in interfaith dialogue. There will be conservative Christians who have no patience with my insistence on understanding, learning, and patience in the area of interfaith dialogue. There will be liberal Christians uncomfortable and in disagreement with my insistence of basic Christian claims about the uniqueness and finality of Jesus Christ. To be clear, my claim is that Jesus Christ is simply the truth—the truth about God and the truth about humanity. Not living into that truth has consequences because this is the last word about God and God's creation. There's nothing more to know. No one apart from Jesus expresses the truth like this. "What the New Testament does not say is, 'unless you hold the following propositions to be true there is no life for you.' What it does say is, 'Without a vital relationship with Jesus Christ who is the word of God made flesh, you will not become what you were made to be. You will not live into your human destiny.'"

4. This is a thesis that deserves a larger treatment. Many Christians seem embarrassed by their own theological education and in embracing pluralism and a host of

other ideas, they seem to have lost the capacity to bear witness. The silence of the Bible from the pulpit has now been joined by the silence of the pew in witness to the uniqueness and finality of Jesus Christ.

5. Rowan Williams: "The finality of Christ in a pluralist world." Christians do not have to give up on the uniqueness and finality of Christ. That's not a useful strategy, and it would be the negation of Pentecost. The church is charged to be witness to the world.

6. Psalm 148. The purpose of the universe is to praise God. This should make us wary of any claims that make less of God's communicative powers.

7. William Sloane Coffin Jr. *Credo*.

12

A Christian Remembrance of Those Who Died in War

Memorial Day 2010

I WANT TO DEDICATE this sermon to Arthur and Catherine Merkle and the yellow cards that they faithfully fill out asking me to pray for our country and especially for our soldiers. These heart-rendered requests deserve a sermon. We will focus on a word that has lost its place in our selfish-oriented, self-centered world: sacrifice.

The word means "to make sacred." And it is only when we treat as sacred the gifts of life, family, church, and nation that we are willing to make sacrifices. If someone produced a sacrifice index that compared Americans' willingness to sacrifice in the 1930s to that of the present, we would see a loss that is injuring our national spirit and strength. John F. Kennedy offered a definition of sacrifice in his inaugural address: "Let every nation know that we shall pay any price, bear any burden, meet any hardship, support any friend, oppose any foe, in order to assure the survival and the success of liberty."

When we send soldiers to war, they pay a price in the loss of the better angels of the human spirit. After all, humans are not natural-born killers. We, being made in the image of God, the God of light, love, and life, were not formed from the dust of the ground as G.I. Joe or G.I. Jane. Humans have to be taught to kill in war.

Lieutenant Colonel Dave Grossman, in his book *On Killing*, outlines the human resistance to killing (commanders from World War II testified that getting three men per squad to fire their rifles was a success and that 15 percent of soldiers fired over the heads of the enemy); the techniques that have been developed in combat training to overcome this resistance; and how the American soldier in Vietnam was psychologically enabled to kill to a far greater degree than any other soldier in history, denied the purification ritual that exists in every warrior society, and finally condemned by his own society. And the tragic price paid by 3,000,000 Vietnam veterans and their families is a crime against our national character.

 Sam Wells tells the story of a Vietnam veteran. An older woman began to verbally attack him: "You got no right to snivel about your little half-baked war. World War II was a real war. I lost a brother in WWII."

 When she wouldn't stop, the veteran looked at her and calmly said: "Have you ever had to kill anyone?"

 "Well, no," she answered belligerently.

 "Then what right have you to tell me anything?" the veteran asked. There was a long, painful silence.

 Then a friend asked the veteran, "When you got pushed just now, you came back with the fact that you had to kill in Vietnam. Was that the worst of it for you?"

 "Yah," he said. "That's half of it."

 After a very long time, the friend asked, "What was the other half?"

 "The other half was that when we got home, nobody understood," the veteran said.

 So a soldier sacrifices to go to war and kill against all his better instincts, "a betrayal," as one soldier put it, "of what I'd been taught as a child," and then he comes back to discover that home treats him as an outcast. I can't help but cry out, "Remorse these veterans need from our country; repentance they need, not self-righteous judgment. Memorial Day is a small expression of our gratitude. One Baptist preacher, whose lottery number was 281, wants to thank our Vietnam veterans.

 Garrison Keillor has a story, as told by Fred Craddock, about being a kid and throwing rocks at pigs that were being slaughtered on his family farm to make the pigs squeal, jump, and run. He thought it was funny.

 "And then I saw my uncle's face inches from mine, and he said, 'If I ever see you do that again, I will beat you until you can't stand up, you hear?'" The sacrifice of the pigs was a ritual, a necessity, and the adults went about their work with little conversation. There was no joking around. Keillor laments that this way of life has disappeared. Death was a part of life. Killing was essential to living. Mankind respected the place of the creatures whose deaths were required for existence. The American Indian asked forgiveness of the spirit of the deer he killed.

"Children growing up in Lake Wobegon will never have a chance to see it. It was a powerful experience, life and death hung in the balance. A life in which people made do, made their own, lived off the land, lived between the ground and God. It's lost, not only to this world, but to memory."

I wish we had a list to read of the names of the soldiers from my church who died serving the United States. I wish we could look at their pictures and imagine all they suffered and sacrificed on our behalf. I have a letter from one of my ancestors, and I take it out and read it from time to time. In my imagination, I try to see this private in the Confederate army named General Kennedy. The letter came from the Battle of Vicksburg and was sent to his mother. His letter testifies that war is hell, and he longs to come home to see his mama. The siege lasted from May 19 until the surrender of the Confederates to General Grant on July 4, 1863. So, on this day, 247 years ago, my cousin faced the charge of a division of Ohio soldiers, and today, I preach a sermon to an Ohio crowd somewhat smaller than a division and a lot friendlier. While I have no use for the cause of the Confederacy, I still feel a connection to General Kennedy. He did what soldiers do: sacrifice for a cause not always understood. An Army chaplain in Iraq says, "It is not a place I would choose to be, but I'm supposed to be here. This is all about taking care of sons and daughters, not about the justice of the cause." In his quarters, this chaplain keeps a supply of children's books and a video camera so parents can read bedtime stories to their children 6,000 miles away.

Our children will never understand, until they have their own children, how many times we have clenched our teeth and carried the load for them. Often without even a hint of gratitude and often with nothing in return but the disrespectful snarls of adolescence, we have sacrificed to give our children every break in the world.

If you have grandchildren, you have a stake in making sure the spirit of sacrifice that made America great survives the current crop of greed-infected, pleasure-obsessed, take-the-shortcut crowd. America can't remain a great nation with people sitting on couches offering blistering criticism of everything anyone tries to accomplish. We watch

"Dancing with the Stars"; our fathers and mothers worked overtime during prime time. Our television stars are judges—from Judge Judy to Doctor Phil to Simon Cowell. Our television idols are "opinionators"—Rachel Maddow, John Stewart, Rush Limbaugh, and Glenn Beck. And this spirit resides not only in those who detest the federal government, but also those who depend on the federal government for everything. As Benjamin Franklin walked out of Constitution Hall, a woman shouted, "What kind of government have you given us?"

"A republic, madam, if you can keep it," Franklin said.

Let us keep it—this land of which Lincoln spoke when he put its unfinished work and future in our hands: "... that we here highly resolve that these dead shall not have died in vain—that this nation, under God, shall have a new birth of freedom—and that government of the people, by the people, for the people, shall not perish from the earth."

Let us make a history—and a her-story—that will make our great-grandchildren proud to be called Americans, a story rooted in sacrifice—actual, sacred, no-joking-around, do-our-job sacrifice.

Last week, I watched a World War II documentary about the American invasion of Okinawa. The Marines went up Sugar Loaf Hill fourteen times before finally securing it. The Second Marine Division was the reserve unit for the invasion, and they were on board ships off the coast of Okinawa—exhausted from taking three islands earlier.

We can't speak of the sacrifices made in war without thinking of another sacrifice on a hill far away, where there stood an old rugged cross, where a man gave his life and made the sacrifice of all sacrifices: the one that justified a desperate world. It is not a sacrifice of killing, but of willing surrender of life. I speak of the sacrifice of Jesus. "No one has greater love than this, to lay down one's life for one's friends."

The death of Jesus on the cross was the actual the "mother of all wars." It was life and love matched against death and hatred, light vs. darkness, goodness vs. wickedness. Jesus won the war, but the victory has not yet been finalized, and to this very day, we are still asking our soldiers to make these awesome sacrifices. And our soldiers keep putting their lives on the line with amazing courage. And so we honor the memory of those who died for us and the courage of those who serve for us in the mountains of Afghanistan and the heart of Iraq.

Their example and the example of Jesus can lead America to return to a principle that has made us a great nation: If we want to live our lives fully, we have to be willing to lay it down, give it away for the sake of others. We must be willing to live for and die for those loved by God. If our world is going to survive the megalomania of rulers in Iran and North Korea, the racial hatred of terrorists like Hamas, Hezbollah, and al-Qaida, the world supremacy illusions of rulers in Communist China, we are going to need someone to lift high the cross.

Every great tradition, as theologian John Cobb suggests, has a universal truth that others should appropriate for themselves and the basic claim of the Christian Gospel: For God so loved the world (a world filled with Jews, Christians, Muslims, Buddhists, Africans, Chinese, Japanese, Hispanics, and a host of others) that God gave the only Son, that whoever believes in him shall not perish but have everlasting life.

Christianity must oppose our popular culture cries for getting what we need, having what we want, and doing as we please. As Peter Marshall said, "The measure of life is its donation, not its duration." It not about the getting, but the giving; not about the selfishness, but the serving; not about the fairness, but the goodness; not about our rights, but the "grace in which we stand." We say thank you for the love of God the Father, Son, and Holy Spirit, and thank you for this human race. As Lady Wisdom puts it, "Rejoicing in God's inhabited world and delighting in the human race." As the psalmist insists: "O Lord, our Sovereign, how majestic is your name in all the earth!"

13

Lessons in Praying from the Jews

JULY 25, 2010

Hosea 1:2–10; Luke 11:1–13

IN THE MOVIE *A Christmas Story*, Flick and Schwartz are daring one another to stick their tongues to a frozen flagpole. Schwartz throws a double-dog-dare. Narrator Ralphie explains, "Now it was serious. What else was there but a 'triple-dare you?'And then, the *coup de grace* of all dares, the sinister 'triple-dog-dare.'"

Then Schwartz unleashes "I triple-dog-dare you." Ralphie reminds the viewer that Schwartz created a slight breach of etiquette by skipping the triple dare and going right for the throat.

Well, in a minor breach of homiletic etiquette, this sermon triple-dog-dares you to pray the Lord's Prayer as if our world depended upon its utterance. It's an argument that the Lord's Prayer is the ultimate speech act of disciples, our real business as Christians. As Martin Luther said, "For to this day, I drink of the Lord's Prayer like a child; drink and eat like an old man; I can never get enough of it. To me it is the best of all prayers."

The Lord's Prayer is not a mantra repeated for Sunday worship, but a *mandate* for us to pray for "a whole new reality, a whole new way of life—a kingdom of God." Missing this, we return to what we mistake for the real world. We go back to being practical. After all, will this prayer restore funds to our depleted pensions? Will it give us jobs and lower taxes? Will this prayer impact the bottom line, bring back our country's prosperity, or revive our cities?

Inhabiting this prayer is to live in Jesus's company, citizen of a new world,[1] the world in which God's rule has arrived but is not yet complete. Inhabiting this prayer transfers us into a world characterized by love of enemies, dependence on God's generosity for daily bread, forgiveness, longing for peace and justice, and patience under attack. To pray like this is to make it real.

The disciples said, "Teach us to pray." After all, they were apprentices of Jesus. And so are we—apprentices to the Master Teacher. Our prayer lives might need a tune-up. Perhaps we are the ones needing to cry out, "Teach us to pray." Regardless of the paradigm or theology involved, no one needs prayer more than apprentices whose vocation is to think, write, teach, preach, witness to, and live the faith.[2]

What does Jesus say? Jesus says, "Pray like this: Your kingdom come." This is our mission statement—the goal toward which we are working. We are praying for a universal kingdom of peace, praise, reconciliation, and delight—not in heaven, but on earth, here and now.

Dare we face a biblical truth? There's no "us vs. them" in the Lord's Prayer; rather: *our* daily bread; *our* sins; do not bring *us* to the time of trial. There's no "them" in the Lord's Prayer, no "this fellow," "those people"; only neighbors. So-called illegal aliens don't need more fences but more friends. If an illegal alien came to your church and needed food and medical care, you wouldn't ask for a green card. You would offer hospitality as surely as Northern Baptists in Ohio offered hospitality to runaway slaves, and as the Jericho prostitute Rahab aided Israel's spies. "Some have entertained angels unaware."[3] Sometimes God's angels look like spies, aliens, slaves. And God's own son, far superior to angels,[4] took the form of a slave.[5]

"It is in the nature of true prayer to remind us of what we may not pray for. We may not ask God for anything that separates us from our neighbor; we cannot ask for 'our daily bread' in such a way as to deny that daily bread to our neighbor. . . . No prayer for private advantage can possibly be directed to the one we call 'Our Father.' God's kingdom cannot come to us apart from our neighbor and still remain God's kingdom."[6] Jesus is us *and* them.

The prophet Hosea says we are a land of whoredom committing great whoredom by forsaking the Lord, but Jesus cleanses us "with the washing of water by the word, so as to present us as a holy and without-blemish bride." And our children are named Lo-ruhamah (Not Pitied),

Lo-ammi (Not my people), but God makes us a chosen race, a royal priesthood, a holy nation, God's own people. "Once you were not a people, but now you are God's people; once you had not received mercy, but now you have received mercy" (1 Peter 2:9–11).

Given our new status and standing, we dare to pray for the kingdom to come, for all the hungry to be fed, for all sins and wrongs to be forgiven, and for salvation from the time of trial. Our prayer is persuasion. Now we dare to haggle with God like Abraham praying for Sodom: "Oh do not let the Lord be angry if I speak just once more. Suppose ten are found there."[7] We dare to pray like Moses reminding God of his own word. "O Lord, you swore to them by your own self, 'I will multiply your descendants like the stars of heaven.'"[8] Abraham and Moses appeal to the deepest and truest thing about God as they pray to him. This is what we can trust about God: generosity at the core of the divine being.

Moses pushes God to the limit. He cries, "If you can't forgive your people, then don't make an exception of me: blot my name out of your book as well."[9] Here is the spirit of the Lord's Prayer: A total lack of self-interest. Therefore, we "approach the throne of grace with boldness and in the name of Jesus and the power of the Holy Spirit demand that no one be left behind, shut out, or turned down.[10]

But there's more: Praying the Lord's Prayer opens the door between earth and heaven to possibilities. God has given us a world where what we do can help or hinder what God achieves in human history. God is in our midst as a constant, active presence. Do not allow human presumption to preclude divine possibilities and miracles.

Buried under layers of highly developed cynicism, we still believe that good triumphs over evil, but in a strange cultural move, we have transferred our hopes from God to pagan mythology: lovable wizards (Harry Potter), handsome vampires, and powerful sorcerers – like Nicholas Cage, the 1,000-year-old sorcerer taught by Merlin. So we flock to good-vs.-evil-themed movies for reassurance that good witches, sorcerers, and vampires will save us from destruction. Robbed of mystery, transcendence, and power, people will go anywhere for some hint of it. Horace Bushnell wrote in the nineteenth century that modern individuals, turned off a rational church, turned to the modern "sorcery" of animal magnetism, spiritualism, and ghosts.[11] What if the church needs a "new heart"[12] to keep vital her intellectual enterprise? Are we all so numbed by our intellectual reduction of God that we no longer see ourselves as involved in a spiritual world beyond our comprehension?[13]

And what does Jesus ask of us? Pray all night long like Jesus in the garden. Pray in agony like Jesus: "If possible let this cup pass from me, but if not, your will be done." Pray like a friend banging on the door at midnight, asking for three loaves of bread. Keep asking until your irritated neighbor gives you not stuff for you but bread for your neighbor. This is not a devotional prayer; it is a desperate prayer. Fling this prayer into the teeth of the darkness, and in the mystery of prayer's reality, the Trinity: Father, Son, and Holy Spirit come alongside to pray with us.

Fred Craddock tells about meeting a seventy-seven year old man named Frank. One day, I met Frank on the street. Then Frank said, "Preacher, I work hard, and I take care of my family, and I mind my own business." So I didn't bother Frank. Then one Sunday morning, Frank presented himself for baptism. Later I asked Frank about how he said, "I mind my own business."

"Yeah," Frank said. "I said it all the time."

"Do you still say that?" I asked.

"Yes," he said.

"Then, what's the difference?" I asked.

"I didn't know then what my business was," Frank said.

This prayer, the Lord's Prayer, is our business: to establish God's kingdom on earth, to give, to serve human need, and to forgive one another. So, I triple dog dare you to test the promises of the one who taught us to pray: "Ask, and the kingdom will be given to you; search and you will find the kingdom; knock, and the door to the kingdom will be opened to you. For everyone who asks receives, and everyone who searches finds, and for everyone who knocks, the door will be opened.

ENDNOTES

1. "So then you are no longer strangers and aliens, but you are citizens with the saints and also members of the household of God, built upon the foundation of the apostles and prophets, with Christ Jesus himself as the cornerstone" (Eph 2:19). "But our citizenship is in heaven, and it is from there that we are expecting a Savior, the Lord Jesus Christ" (Phil 3:20). "Beloved, I urge you as aliens and exiles to abstain from the desires of the flesh that wage war against the soul" (1 Pet 2:11).

2. "Pray in the Spirit at all times in every prayer and supplication. To that end keep alert and always persevere in supplication for all the saints. Pray also for me, so that when I speak, a message may be given to me to make known with boldness the mystery of the gospel, for which I am an ambassador in chains. Pray that I may declare it boldly as I must speak" (Eph 6:18–20).

3. Heb 13:1–2.
4. Heb 1:1–13.
5. Phil 2:5–11.
6. Theodore W. Jennings Jr. *Life as Worship: Prayer in Jesus' Name.*
7. Gen 19.
8. Exod 32:11–14.
9. Exod 32:32.
10. "I have great sorrow and unceasing anguish in my heart. For I could wish that I myself were accursed and cut off from Christ for the sake of my own people, my kindred according to the flesh" (Rom 9:2–3).
11. Robert Mullin, in *Miracles and the Modern Religious Imagination*, argues that the Protestant insistence that miracles stopped at the end of the biblical period succeeded in making skeptics of us all, removing even the possibility of the miraculous.
12. See Jer 31:31–34.
13. No matter how much we know, some days we have to simply stand next to Job: "Therefore, I have uttered what I did not understand, things too wonderful for me, which I did not know. I had heard of you by the hearing of the ear, but now my eye sees you; therefore I repent in dust and ashes." (Job 42:3–6).

14

Jesus as Trouble

AUGUST 15, 2010

Luke 12:49–56

JESUS: SPELL HIS NAME "Trouble." The words in Luke are loaded with trouble: fire, baptism, stress, division, and eight times the word "against." A Baptist deacon voted the same way on every issue: "I'm agin' it, preacher." His whole existence was an encyclopedia of being against. Well, in America, "being against" is a growth industry. It pays well; you get to be on television; and you don't have to do any actual work.

Well Jesus was all the trouble in the world from the outset. At his dedication in the temple, all of eight days young, Jesus caused a prophetic outburst: "This child is destined for the falling and rising of many in Israel." Trouble.

As a baby, Jesus haunted the dreams of Herod, who ordered the killing of all boys under the age of two in Bethlehem. Trouble.

As a twelve-year-old boy, he worried his parents: "I must be about my Father's business." Trouble.

At his hometown synagogue of Nazareth, he enraged the congregation by insisting that God cared for foreigners. They tried to kill him for that sermon. Trouble.

Jesus was trouble from the outset.

As a teacher, he got under the skin of every religious/political group in Palestine.[1] Jesus had little patience with the Pharisees, religious strict constructionists; the Sadducees, first-century equivalents of television evangelists, who turned the Temple into a den of thieves; the Herodians, a "downtown luncheon club" aligned with the powerful elite of the city; the Essenes who left town years before, refusing to have anything to do with politics; the Zealots, super patriotic conspiracy masters and violence lovers. Trouble.

But haven't times changed? Jesus isn't trouble today, is he? Haven't we made him so easy that everyone can believe in him and ignore him all at once? But what does Jesus say to us? "I have come to bring division." He was talking about families divided over faith, but today, Jesus offends our cultural sensitivities. Good heavens, all along we have been thinking of faith as an easygoing compromise with the world—where no one is offended, and every truth claim gets equal billing.[2] We aren't asking for stars in a crown, but shouldn't we get a pat on the back for being so agreeable? Instead, "I came to bring fire and division to the earth." We are shocked.

Now, do we see the little game we've been playing? Have you ever taken your granddaughter to the American Girl store? You can order a doll that looks just like you. Well, welcome to the American Jesus store: Make Jesus look like you, talk like you, think like you. In the delightful novel *Raney*, Charles, college librarian and Episcopalian, and Raney, small-town Baptist girl, are a newly married couple. They get into a fight over Jesus. Charles says, "Raney, Jesus Christ was a radical. If the people in Bethel Free Will Baptist met Jesus they'd laugh at him . . . or lynch him." "A radical? Charles, I had a personal experience with Jesus Christ when I was twelve years old. He wasn't a radical then. And I didn't laugh. As a matter of fact, I cried." "Were you saved, Raney? Is that it? Were you saved and now you're going to heaven and nothing else matters?" "Charles, you can run down whoever and whatever you want to, but you run down my experience of Jesus Christ you are putting yourself below the belly of a hog." Raney went to the bedroom and slammed the door with both hands as hard as she could. Charles stomped out of the house and drove off. He didn't come back for thirty minutes. Divided family. Jesus was and is trouble.

Is that what we've been up to around here? We think Jesus thinks like us, believes like us, and blesses all we do. Jesus is a commodity, a symbol, a flag to run up the pole. Perhaps this is why Jesus appears to matter so much more in America than in Europe. Here, we use Jesus for every political and social cause.

Almost everyone has opinions about Jesus. Movie makers, novelists, newspaper columnists, the garden variety atheist, the comic writers of *South Park*, the television opinionator. People just think they know Jesus, but they are suspicious of the Jesus specialists. If you had cancer, you'd see an oncologist; depression, a psychiatrist; tax issues, a CPA; legal problems, a lawyer. But in our amazingly anti-intellectual culture, the one person who can't seem to be trusted with Jesus is the Christian theologian, who has given his or her life to the study of Scripture, theology, philosophy, and ethics, and who clings to a faith informed by Scripture, history, and tradition.[3]

"I believe in one Lord Jesus Christ, the only-begotten Son of God, begotten of his Father before all worlds, God of God, light of light, very God of very God."

"Boring," shouts our world.

But it makes a lot more sense to me than the theory that Jesus was a great teacher who gave good advice.[4]

Listen, if you want good advice for prosperous living, listen to Joel Osteen. But if you want a gospel that's tough enough and trouble enough to survive our kind of world, let me recommend that you give the real Jesus another chance—"the one who lived a human life and had a human will whose power and joy was the perfect performance of who God is and what God wants, the performance of the Word of God."[5]

Now, perhaps, dimly, we start to understand. Jesus refuses to fit our agenda. Jesus is not a candidate or a sponsor. He's not on a side. He was never a member of Moral Majority; they crucified him as a member of the immoral minority—between two thieves. Faith is not about Jesus joining our side; it is about us following Jesus. Jesus may not be on our side. Let me say this again: Jesus may not be on our side.

New Testament scholar E. P. Sanders reminds us that today's story of families divided over faith was a later church issue. Known as "retrojection," this method takes an issue and puts it back in the time of Jesus and allows Jesus to speak with authority to the church about the issue.

I'm asking that you join me in a single project: Take our troubling issues and overlay them with the words of Jesus. Let Jesus, who we assume is present with us, lead the way as we discern the purpose of life. We have Jesus, and we have Scripture, and we have all these troublesome issues. Let's work with the material we have. Let us run the race that is set before us, looking to Jesus the pioneer and perfecter of our faith.

ENDNOTES

1. It is a mistake to assume that these groups are anything other than representatives of society, culture, politics, and life in any age, including our own. These are our kind of people. This eliminates the prospect of anti-Semitism and also gives the Gospel story a chance at transforming our lives rather than us simply continuing to act as if the Pharisees et al. are the ultimate and only enemies of Jesus.

2. Religion is not a private affair, and it is not just individualistic. If religion is private and for the individual only, pretty soon there will be no religious conversation. There's an anxiety among believers that we lack the words to describe our faith in public. In the short story "Personal Testimony," a twelve-year-old daughter of a minister makes hundreds of dollars at a Baptist summer camp running "a ghost-writing service for Jesus," composing for other campers the personal testimonies of conversion they are expected to give. We have actually grown comfortable with this amazing silence, this complete lack of a faith language in our daily lives. As Flip Wilson once said, "I'm a Jehovah's Bystander. They wanted me to be a Jehovah's Witness, but I don't want to be involved."

3. See Terry Eagleton, *Reason, Faith, and Revolution: Reflections on the God Debate*. Eagleton challenges the new atheism of Richard Dawkins and Christopher Hitchens. He even conflates their names into one name, "Ditchkins," and then skewers them both as spokespersons of the new atheism. But this is not the usual response even among the churches. We give the new atheists too much credit. There is a persecution of Christian faith by secular, materialistic, intellectuals. They pour so much scorn on belief in God and make such fun of believers. And their intellectual gravitas is so accepted, their professional vitae so honored, and their intelligence so prized, that thousands of ordinary citizens buy their arguments without carefully checking them out. For example, how many of you are aware that the arguments of Dawkins and Hitchens are against believing in a notion of God that was alive in the nineteenth century, but one which no believer embraces today?

4. Are we really determined to be part of a Christian movement that marginalizes Jesus so that he becomes merely a quizzical teacher of wisdom, to be ranged alongside other quizzical teachers of wisdom, from many traditions? No reason emerges as to why we should take this teacher any more or less seriously than any other. It is not clear why even a sustained attempt to follow his maxims, his isolated aphorisms, should offer hope in a world threatened by ecological disasters, nuclear holocausts, resurgent tribalisms—and, for those insulated from such things in certain parts of the Western world, the moral and spiritual bankruptcy of materialism. The whole point of calling Gospels "Gospels" was, I suggest, that they did contain reason for hope, good news to a world that badly needed it. If we persist in our distancing ourselves from Jesus, we are systematically deconstructing our own faith. If Jesus really is just a wise rabbi, a great teacher, and an inspiring role model, then there is no Gospel, no good news. There is only good advice, and we have no reason for thinking that it will have any effect. From a historical point of view, it might of course be true that there is no good news to be had. Christianity as a whole might simply have been whistling in the dark for 2,000 years. Subversive aphorisms may be the only comfort, the only hope we have. But I seriously doubt that is so.

5. Rowan Williams, *Tokens of Trust*.

15

Worship: A Sunday Choice

OCTOBER 10, 2010

Luke 17:11–19

ON 10/10/10 WE HAVE a text with ten lepers calling, "Have mercy." It's a veritable mob of human need:

- A senior citizen battling the killing pain of arthritis, the debilitating results of a stroke, diabetes, or cancer. Have mercy.
- Parents struggling to keep a child from failure or out of drugs. Have mercy.
- A couple battling to save their home and running out of savings. Have mercy.

We have all this human need, and I think it takes a lot of gall to say that we are a bunch of do-gooders or bleeding hearts because we believe God has ordained us to meet all this human need. We are our brothers' and sisters' keepers. We are the Good Samaritans. "Have mercy" can't be ignored.

What does Jesus do when he hears? This is crucial because however Jesus responds to cries for mercy is the way we are supposed to respond.

Jesus passed out mercy. Isn't that just like him? Jesus never said no to a cry for mercy: a father with an epileptic son; a mother with a emotionally spent daughter; two blind men from Jericho who rushed up to Jesus and said, "Lord, have mercy."[1] Goodness and mercy followed Jesus all the days of his life. There's no such thing as too much mercy. We are God's mercy-dripping, mercy-granting, mercy-doing people.

And no matter what postmodernists say, there is a grand drama of mercy in the fabric of our being. We have been given roles in the drama. Did you think you were just part of an audience gathered at church to offer your opinion about the quality of the sermon or your critique about the singing? Not on your life. You got the part. You are a member of the chorus of those in whose lives the glory of God is revealed. This is not a bit part. You have a starring role. Spread the goodness and mercy.

Show mercy, and God receives glory. Sometimes, a stubborn church gets it wrong and thinks God gets glory when we throw our moral weight around, when we judge and condemn others. It's the dark side of the church. We see it in the treatment of lepers. The biblical law was explicit: Cast them out of the camp. They were required to wear torn clothes, and as they walked on the street they had to cry out, "Unclean, unclean."[2]

Bad religion is a hard habit to break, and after fifteen centuries of knowing that Jesus touched lepers, loved lepers, healed lepers, invited lepers into the community of faith, the stubborn, unbending, cold church still couldn't break its nasty habit. The church in the fourteenth century had a service called the Mass of Separation. *The whole parish accompanied a newly identified leper to his/her new home as the priest performed the Mass:* "I forbid you to ever enter a church, a monastery, a fair, a mill, a market, or an assembly of people. I forbid you to leave your house unless dressed in your recognizable garb."[3]

I bet there were good church people of the time who said, "I don't have anything against lepers as long as they stay in their place." Please note that *place* is a highly charged emotional and political metaphor. Lepers had a place: outside the camp. Women had a place: in the kitchen. African-Americans had a place: on the other side of the tracks or the river. Gays had a place: in the closet. Illegal immigrants had a place: Mexico. The homeless have a place: out of sight. Once, New York City's mayor got rid of homeless people. He simply moved them to New Jersey. So the place for New York homeless: Anywhere in New Jersey. We use place to exclude people from their rightful place.

Medicine finally eliminated leprosy, but religion retains its voracious appetite for excluding, judging, condemning people. Lepers have at various times been replaced by Jews, Catholics, African-Americans, women, gays, immigrants, anyone who is different. In Mentor, Ohio, a sixteen-year-old girl committed suicide. The native Croatian was mocked for her accent, had food thrown on her and was called names. It was the fourth time in little more than two years that a bullied high school student in this small Cleveland suburb on Lake Erie died by his or her own hand—three suicides, one overdose of antidepressants. One was bullied for being gay, another for having a learning disability, another for being a boy who happened to like wearing pink. My friend Rabbi Sofian tells me that his community has a queasy feeling about the environment in our country. And if anyone knows about persecution, it is the Jewish community. Tell me, isn't the image of the church as moral bully a blasphemous monster?

Can God's people finally learn our lesson from a healed and converted Samaritan leper—a man doubly excluded, now healed and saved? Pour these words in concrete at the entryway to your heart: God receives glory through mercy—act after act of mercy.[4] Pile on the mercy. There's no such thing as too much mercy coming from the church.

Jesus, having mercy, healed all ten lepers. Nine of them quickly disappear. They make only a cameo appearance in the drama. They were not grateful, but Jesus heals indiscriminately.

But look! One turned back to Jesus Christ. Turning back is a term of conversion. Is Luke showing us how a person joins the church? The leper turned back and started "praising God with a loud voice."

The psalmist says, "Let us make a joyful noise to God; sing the glory of his name; give to God glorious praise." God receives glory from our praises. After all, isn't that how glory spreads? We repeat the stories of prodigious feats. This is how God's reputation is enhanced in the world. A major part of our witness is praising God. Of course we think of praising God as singing hymns, but it is practice for our praise work during the week. We leave church and praise God to a skeptical world.

Recently, the U.S. Supreme Court heard the case of the Rev. Fred Phelps and his band of protestors. His little group holds up a sign at funerals of American soldiers: "God hates fags." This is where there must be a wall of praise raised against Rev. Phelps. The name of God doesn't belong in the same sentence with the word hate.[5] John says, "God is love."[6] We should surround Rev. Phelps with a million Christians waving signs: "God is love." Smother this angry little preacher in mercy, grace, and goodness. Praise is a way of proclaiming the reputation of God, and when we praise God, we give God glory.

Look, there's more: The healed leper thanked Jesus. When he said thank you, the Samaritan entered a whole new world.

May we learn once again the power of "thank you." I'm talking about the kind of person you become when you express gratitude. It is a practice that makes you a better person—a person you will really like a lot. Say thank you to the person who serves your food, to the person who holds the door open for you, to the person who bags your groceries, to the person who brings you a dozen pair of shoes to try on at the mall. Say thank you to your parents, for goodness' sake. Say thank you to the teachers who struggle so mightily to teach your "perfect" children. Saying thank you saves us from the cynicism, mistrust, suspicion, and skepticism of our world.

Sam Wells, chaplain at Duke University, tells the story of Martin Rinkart, a pastor of the German town of Eilenberg in 1618 just as the Thirty Years' War was beginning. Political and military refugees flocked to the walled town of Eilenberg. Disease and famine wreaked havoc in the town. In 1637, there was a terrible plague. Pastor Rinkart, who had lost half of his household, including his wife, was the only pastor remaining in Eilenberg. He conducted 4,000 funerals in that year, sometimes up to 50 funerals a day. This pastor could have been forgiven for feeling resentful, angry, and unforgiving, but he sat down and wrote one of the most famous hymns of Germany, which we know as "Now Thank We All Our God." In writing this hymn, he displayed what we rediscover when we sing it today: the power of saying thank you.

Now, do we get it? We have a role to play: Giving mercy in a world filled with need. Praising God in a world that is filled with cussing. Saying thank you to everyone. That's our part. Let's perform it to the max.

ENDNOTES

1. Matt 17:15. How many fathers join me this morning in pleading for our children, "Lord have mercy." A Canaanite woman cried, "Have mercy on me, O Lord; my daughter is severely possessed by a demon" (Matt 15:22). Two blind men from Jericho cried, "Have mercy on us." The crowd rebuked the blind men and told them to shut up. The crowd opposed Jesus granting mercy, but Jesus doesn't listen much to crowds (Matt 20:30).

2. Num 5:2-3 makes it so clear: "Command the people of Israel that they put out of the camp every leper, and every one having a discharge, and every one that is unclean through contact with the dead; you shall put them outside the camp, that they may not defile their camp, in the midst of which I dwell." Compare Hebrews 13:13-16: "Therefore let us go forth to him outside the camp and bear the abuse he endured.

Through him let us continually offer up a sacrifice of praise to God, that is, the fruit of lips that acknowledge his name. Do not neglect to do good and to share what you have, for such sacrifices are pleasing to God."

3. "I forbid you to wash your hands or to launder anything or to drink at any stream or fountain, unless using your own barrel or dipper. I forbid you to touch anything you buy or barter for, until it becomes your own. I forbid you to enter any tavern; and if you wish for wine, whether you buy it or it is given to you, have it funneled into your keg. I forbid you to share house with any woman but your wife. I command you, if accosted by anyone while travelling on a road, to set yourself down-wind of them before you answer. I forbid you to enter any narrow passage, lest a passerby bump into you. I forbid you, wherever you go, to touch the rim or the rope of a well without donning your gloves. I forbid you to touch any child or give them anything. I forbid you to drink or eat from any vessel but your own."

4. Mercy is rooted in God's covenant-keeping faithfulness, God's willingness to keep working with stubborn and failing people. The Greek word for mercy is *eleos,* and it belongs to the genre of *pathos,* the emotion aroused by contact with an affliction that comes undeservedly on someone else. Its lowest common denominator is pity or sympathy. But it is more than an attitude; it is a helpful act. The Hebrew word is *chesed* and always denotes God's faithful and merciful help. In the New Testament, *eleos* is the word used for the divinely required attitude of people to people. It is a mercy that is concerned for both physical need as well as the eternal welfare of others.

5. The only places in Scripture that I could find where it says anything about God hating are Ps 11 and Mal 1:3. Ps 11 is a dubious theological claim rather than a statement by God: "His soul hates him that loves violence." Mal 1:3 has God say, "I have hated Esau." Prov 6:16 says God hates haughty eyes, a lying tongue, hands that shed innocent blood, a heart that devises wicked plans, feet that make haste to run to evil, a false witness who breathes out lies, and a man who sows discord among brothers." Wicked deeds: Hos 9:15. Amos 5:21 says God hates bad worship.

6. John also says, "If any one has the world's goods and sees his brother in need, yet closes his heart against him, how does God's love abide in him? Little children, let us not love in word but in deed and in truth."

16

Thanksgiving: Are We Still Pilgrims?

*Deuteronomy 26:1–11; Psalm 100;
Philippians 4:4–9; John 6:25–35*

"L ET'S TALK TURKEY."
It means to speak plainly about a difficult or awkward subject, or it may refer to pleasant chitchat. Or the actual sounds a turkey makes.

Turkey gobbling was a distinct, natural sound on frontier farms, so to "talk turkey" meant to skip the pleasantries and get to what's important. So let's skip the small talk and get to the big talk.

Language is so crucial to the human experience. Linguists estimate that there are 6,809 "living" languages in the world today; 90 percent of them are spoken by fewer than 100,000 people; 46 are known to have just one native speaker. That gives a whole new meaning to talking to yourself.

"There are 357 languages with under 50 speakers," says Bill Sutherland, a population biologist.[1] "People just don't want to learn a language because they know there are so few others who can speak it. A language can disappear, and once it is gone, it can't be recovered."

There's one particular language that concerns me. While it doesn't belong to the official family of languages, I call it the language of Thanksgiving. In our polyglot, rude, ill-mannered culture, this language is in danger of disappearing. So, do you speak Thanksgiving?

We can't speak Thanksgiving without learning the language of the Native Americans. The school version of the Thanksgiving story is an incomplete tale. Bill Trollinger argues that we can and should make Thanksgiving a more "profoundly spiritual holiday."[2] That entails remembering that in the years just prior to the arrival of the Pilgrims, diseases brought by Europeans ravaged Native American tribes in New England. An estimated 80 million out of 100 million Native Americans in North and South America died of disease in what historians call the greatest demographic disaster of all time. The Puritans would not have survived without the assistance they received from Native Americans.[3] We would be glossing over the meaning of Thanksgiving without reminding you that the harmony between Pilgrims and Indians ended just over a year after the first Thanksgiving.

We should celebrate Thanksgiving with the recognition that our country was built upon foundations laid by native peoples. We should approach Thanksgiving in a celebratory mood that is tempered by a "spirit of sadness and repentance acknowledging that the first Thanksgiving is an ideal that we as a nation and we as Christians have too rarely realized."[4] Remember: Ideals can be a spur to greatness or a sickness that produces hard-core, blind ideology.

The language of Thanksgiving is incomprehensible without learning the language of the Pilgrims. A group of English separatists, "Puritans with a vengeance," set sail on the Mayflower seeking a land of religious freedom. The voyage took sixty-five days. They lived in between the deck and the hold, a crawl space not more than five feet high. They brought food, water, firewood, and beer—all of which was either gone or nearly gone before the trip was over.[5]

They knew the danger. By the time the Pilgrims set sail, 3,000 of the 3,600 English colonists at Jamestown had died. Yes, they knew the danger. But they fervently believed God wanted them to do this and would provide for them.

"We verily believe and trust the Lord is with us and will graciously prosper our endeavor," they wrote. Their leader, William Bradford, said, "They knew they were Pilgrims."

Fifty-two of the 102 died the first winter. With the aid of friendly Native Americans, they planted their first crops that spring. By September, they had corn, squash, beans, peas, and barley (which meant they could have beer). William Bradford wrote, "They gathered the fruits of their labors: it is time to rejoice together after a more special manner." This is the feast we now celebrate as Thanksgiving. The Native Americans arrived, bringing five freshly killed deer. So the feast included vegetables, geese, ducks, wild turkey, venison, striped bass, bluefish, cod, and whiskey. It was a veritable Puritan feast—not an oxymoron. There were no mashed potatoes.

With the odds stacked so severely, they should have all been dead by spring.

"Their survival was a testament to their grit, resolve, and faith." They knew they were pilgrims. They were tough and willing to "screw their courage to the sticking point when their time came." Some Christians are soft-headed; from time to time they read their Commandments wrong and weaken in the faith. But note these English separatists. They were pilgrims. Do we know that we are Pilgrims still? Are we a people undeterred by unspeakable odds? In 2 Chronicles 14:9, we read, "Zerah the Ethiopian came out against Judah with an army of a million men." Talk about bad odds. King Asa didn't back down: "Help us, O Lord our God, for we rely on you, and in your name we have come against this multitude." They were a people with a mission more than a home. "The Lord said to Abram, 'Go from your father's house to the land that I will show you.' So Abram went." These were a people on a journey, not a cruise—a people who live by hope; a people who will risk life and limb for a cause greater than their own; a people who keep fighting battles we thought were already won. A people prepared to pay any price, give any gift, and do any work to carry out this mission.

The writers of Scripture can teach us the language of Thanksgiving. The story of the first Jewish Thanksgiving is in our Deuteronomy reading: "A wandering Aramean was my ancestor. The Lord brought us out of Egypt with a mighty hand and gave us this land, a land flowing with milk and honey. So now I bring the first fruit of the ground, that you, O Lord have given me." There is a sense that the Psalter—a collection of hymns and poems—is the continued story of Thanksgiving: "O give thanks to the Lord, call on his name, make known his deeds among the peoples" (Psalm 105:1). "Enter the gates of God with thanksgiving, and his courts with praise.

We can't live a story we don't know or speak a language we don't live and practice.

The poets can help us speak the language of Thanksgiving: gratitude for the gift of life, of every day, of every moment as precious. Thanksgiving is a language of possibilities. The poet Wallace Stevens: "It is possible, possible, possible. It must be possible. It must be that in time the real from its rude compounding come. . . . To be stripped of every fiction except one. The fiction of an absolute."

Poetry gives us the sense of what is possible and rescues us from a flat, reduced, trivial prose. Each dawn is charged with possibilities, each Lord's Day with a new beginning wrapped in forgiveness. When I open a new ream of paper, 500 bright, white, empty sheets, I hold them next to my ear and use my thumb to flutter the pages and think of all the possible words that will soon fill those pages.

Come to a poetry reading and learn that every day is Thanksgiving, that a day without Thanksgiving is a poorly lived day. If we don't share, if we don't give thanks, we will not notice that we are alive. Hear poetry as the human spirit's resistance to technology, which often can reduce life to robotic repetition and meaningless work.

Here's Jane Kenyon, one of my favorite poets:

> I got out of bed
> on two strong legs.
> It might have been
> otherwise. I ate
> cereal, sweet
> milk, ripe, flawless
> peach. It might
> have been otherwise.
> I took the dog uphill
> to the birch wood.
> All morning I did
> the work I love.
>
> At noon I lay down
> with my mate. It might
> have been otherwise.
> We ate dinner together
> at a table with silver
> candlesticks. It might
> have been otherwise.
> I slept in a bed
> in a room with paintings
> on the walls, and
> planned another day
> just like this day.
> But one day, I know,
> it will be otherwise.

Here's Mary Oliver, in her poem "The Summer Day":

> Who made the world?
> Who made the swan, and the black bear?
> Who made the grasshopper?
> This grasshopper, I mean—
> the one who has flung herself out of the grass,
> the one who is eating sugar out of my hand,
> who is moving her jaws back and forth instead of up and down—
> who is gazing around with her enormous and complicated eyes.
> Now she lifts her pale forearms and thoroughly washes her face.
> Now she snaps her wings open, and floats away.
> I don't know exactly what a prayer is.
> I do know how to pay attention, how to fall down
> into the grass, how to kneel down in the grass,
> how to be idle and blessed, how to stroll through the fields,
> which is what I have been doing all day.
> Tell me, what else should I have done?
> Doesn't everything die at last, and too soon?
> Tell me, what is it you plan to do
> with your one wild and precious life?

Pattiann Rogers, in her poem "The Greatest Grandeur":

> But it is the dark emptiness contained
> in every next moment that seems to me
> the most singularly glorious gift,
> that void which one is free to fill
> that space large enough to hold all
> invented blasphemies and pieties, 10,000
> definitions of god and more, never fully filled, never.

The poets singing their songs are a renewable spiritual resource against technology's dulling, deadening impact on our souls. God isn't a character in our lives; God is the plot.

Thus, the true poet.[6]

For Christians, the true poet is the one who came unto his own, singing his song: "The kingdom of God is here and now, in this one moment," the one who was rich and for sake became poor, the one who emptied himself taking the form of a slave, the one who became obedient to the point of death—even death on a cross, the one through whom God was pleased to reconcile all things, this Jesus, whom I declare to you is the primary speaker of Thanksgiving. He is the most crucial renewable spiritual resource in the world. When we give God thanks and praise and pass bread and wine, we offer the world the one who promised, "Whoever comes to me will never be hungry, and whoever believes in me will never be thirsty" (John 6:35). It is the language of Jesus that finally saves us from the American civil religion and its overcooked romanticism. Jesus gives us the reason for Thanksgiving that matters most of all.

Sure, we are going through a rough spot, but the best time to speak Thanksgiving is in adverse times. When you are between a rock and a hard place, speak Thanksgiving. When you are at the end of your rope, speak Thanksgiving; when difficult people have stepped on your last nerve, speak Thanksgiving. First thing in the morning, start your day saying, "My God, it is good to be alive."

The Methodists have a tradition of singing a hymn at the end of their annual conference. It's a Charles Wesley song, "And Are We Yet Alive?" The first verse goes like this:

> And are we yet alive,
> And see each other's face?
> Glory and praise to Jesus give
> For his redeeming grace.

My God, it is good to be alive.
Happy Thanksgiving.

ENDNOTES

1. Bill Sutherland, "Alarm Raised on World's Disappearing Languages," 2003. Sutherland is a population biologist.

2. William Vance Trollinger Jr., "The First Thanksgiving: The Rest of the Story."

3. We should also make sure that we include the experiences of Squanto as a case study of the negative effects of European expansion upon native peoples. Squanto was captured and shipped overseas to be sold into slavery. Somehow he escaped and landed in England, where he learned to speak English. Then in 1619 he was employed as a guide for an expedition to New England, and he returned home. In 1621, he came to Plymouth and offered his services to the Pilgrims. He taught them a host of survival skills.

4. Trollinger, "The First Thanksgiving: The Rest of the Story."

5. Nathaniel Philbrick, *Mayflower: A Story of Courage, Community, and War.*

6. Walt Whitman: "Finally shall come the poet worthy of the name, the true son of god shall come singing his songs." Of course Whitman has a different poet in mind than I do, but the poetry allows me to give a different meaning.

17

When the Preacher Is Depressed
December 12, 2010

Matthew 11:2-12; Isaiah 35:1-10

With the calendar showing a scant 13 days to Christmas, imagine getting a phone call: The preacher is in jail. Now, that would make the newspaper—front page.

That's how it must have been when people learned that their very own John the Baptist, the preacher of Advent, was in jail.

John's disciples struggled with the news, all of them talking at once. Imagine what they were saying:

> John's in jail. Have you heard? Herod locked John in jail. I heard that he threw away the key. My cousin, who lives in Jerusalem, tells me Herod's wife wants his head on a platter. I heard she's the meanest woman in the Roman Empire. God bless her.

No one knows what to do: the preacher is in jail.

John's disciples remember those early days when the whole region was singing John's praise. Imagine what they heard:

> What a great preacher. Some folks claim he's the promised Messiah. I went down to the River Jordan every day and counted all those people who came out to hear our preacher preach. John baptized me. I will never forget it as long as I live.

John's in jail, worrying about his congregation, but even more disturbing: He's depressed. John grew up in the wilderness, and now he is in Herod's hole in the ground. I bet, like Geronimo, the great Apache chief imprisoned at Fort Sill, he wore a trench in the dirt floor of that cell pacing back and forth. Prison is no place for a preacher like John.

Jail or not, something in us rebels at the idea of a depressed preacher. Truth is, we often have unrealistic expectations of preachers. We shouldn't be surprised that depression among clergy is so high. An article in *The New York Times* August 2, 2010, noted, "Members of the clergy now suffer from obesity, hypertension and depression at rates higher than most Americans. In the last decade, their use of antidepressants has risen, while their life expectancy has fallen. Many would change jobs if they could." A wise pastor once told me, "When the president makes a mistake, when Congress acts shamefully, there are people who will blame you because they know you and you answer your phone. They will say, 'Preacher, do something.' Don't let that throw you. Have some compassion. You are their pastor, and they need to vent."

John the Baptist starts out preaching up a storm. After thirty years of wilderness training, John sweeps into town. Even Jesus was impressed: "What did you expect? "Someone dressed in soft robes? Look, those who wear soft robes are in palaces." John baptized Jesus, called him the Lamb of God, taking away the sins of the world. John expected a parade, not a prison. And therein lies the trouble.

John's depression is related to his expectations: "Are you the one, or should we look for another?"

We understand. A wife says, "He's not the man I thought he was." A teacher says, "I'm so disappointed in your performance." A parent says, "I didn't spend $30,000 a year for you to make D's." Expectations, starting as wild dreams, can turn into nightmares. One of our presidents was elected because the image makers did a wonderful job, but in the process they oversold him. Before taking office, this president told a newspaper editor that he feared "the exaggerated idea the people have conceived of me. They have a conviction that I'm some sort of superman. If some calamity should come upon the nation, I would be sacrificed to the unreasoning disappointment of a people who expected too much." The year was 1928, and the president was Herbert Hoover. The calamity was the Great Depression. It's a challenge to navigate between expecting too much and expecting too little. Expectations can be a devil.

Some Christians have a tendency to give up too soon. We count seconds and minutes; God counts centuries and eons. "Should we look for another?" Jesus has only been working for about two months when

John sends his impatient word. We try to make Jesus be like us instead of allowing Jesus to make us like him. Secretly, I bet some of us expect more from God. After all, we are faithful church members. Don't we come to church, give, sing, pray? Like Esau, we cry, "Father don't you have a blessing for me?" Expectations can get out of control and wreak havoc with our faith.

John expected an axe-wielding Jesus, a burn-it-all-to-the-ground Jesus; instead he got, "Rise, take up your pallet, and walk." He got, "Lazarus, come forth." He got, "Go in peace. Your sins are forgiven." John couldn't have felt less powerful.

The ministry can feel so powerless. Some memories never leave me: A three year old boy dies from meningitis. A twenty-one year old college student stabbed to death. A sixteen-year-old girl dies while I'm holding her hand and praying for her healing. A thirty-eight year old multimillionaire commits suicide, and his wife asks me, "Why did this happen? We had everything. Three beautiful children. A gorgeous home. All this money. Why, preacher, why?" I have always been helped by the words of a famous preacher, who in his first sermon after the death of his wife, said, "Some people tell me I should fling away my faith. Fling away to what?" Faith, if we will follow, can help us out of the prison of depression.

When expectations fail, we enter a danger zone. Matthew 11:12 is critical to understanding our predicament. "From the days of John the Baptist until now the kingdom of heaven has suffered violence, and the violent take it by force." Nothing is more dangerous than religious expectations gone astray. First thing you know, some Anglican named Darby is dreaming up Jesus rapturing the church and destroying the world—a violent scenario, a nasty perversion. The church is more likely to be ruptured than raptured.

When some people of faith are disappointed by poor results, they drop Jesus and take things into their own hands. The kingdom of heaven is vulnerable to human violence based on human impatience and lust for false power. The irony is that by taking the kingdom by violence, we destroy it. (Note: In the King James Version, verse 12 reads, "The violent bear the kingdom away.)

Coercion, force, intimidation, anger, guilt inducement—all these are church forms of violence. It is a form of violence to force our Christian convictions on people. Jesus has not called us to control Washington, D.C., but to renew it—save it, even. Jesus has not called us to be religious vigilantes bent on making sure that everybody who has it coming gets it.

Much that we call church has become a violent place. People push a certain reading of Scripture down our throats. I received an evaluation from a University of Dayton Lifelong Learning student: "Dr. Kennedy needs to believe in the rapture, or he is going to hell." What disturbed my student so much? I taught that Jesus would come back the same way he came the first time—not with an army but with a choir of angels; forgiving sin, not fomenting revolution. Rapture is an extreme makeover of Jesus from Lamb of God to warrior of destruction. Wrong.

Well, Jesus does have an answer for John. "Go and tell John what you hear and see." What about us? What are people hearing and seeing from the church today? In my mind's eye, I saw a box filled with the words and deeds of what has become the fussing, fighting, feuding church of Jesus. Politics. A literal Bible. Women priests. Gay marriage. Abortion. The environment. Bearing weapons. Creationism against evolution. Bigotry. Immigration. Patriotism. I even found a seminary president raising sand about yoga. And at the bottom of the box, I found this old book.

There was a little dust on the cover, but I didn't let that fool me about what was inside. In my mind's ear, an angel whispered that I should open the book and read what I found: "The blind receive their sight, the lame walk, the lepers are cleansed, the deaf hear, the dead are raised, and the poor have good news brought to them." Perhaps the grouping of resurrection and good news for the poor means that it will take a power as great as resurrection to get Americans to actually care for the poor.

The answer Jesus gives is the answer Isaiah gave before him: "Then the eyes of the blind shall be opened, and the ears of the deaf unstopped; then the lame shall leap like a deer, and the tongue of the speechless sing for joy." "Strengthen the weak hands, and make firm the feeble knees. Be strong; do not fear! Here is your God." And the answer James gives: "Be patient, therefore, beloved, until the coming of the Lord." Wait for it. Work for it. Stick with the program.

The answer Jesus gives says that the kingdom is coming from a bunch of sinners with enough sense to repent—not a bunch of holy people waving Bibles and passing legislation. Can't we get it through our heads and into our hearts that Jesus comes to the little people, not the big shots? The poor, not the rich? The weak, not the strong?

From time to time, one or two finally get it and take up the call of sacrificing, suffering, loving commitment.

Many are called, but few stick it out. The churches are filled with members, but disciples are few. First one, then another will act, and their actions will signal the beginning of a great movement of renewal where the shelf life of selfishness expires, and the stranglehold of greed on the American psyche will be broken. Scattered across the stories of the New Testament are examples of those who got it:

- "You are the Christ, the Son of the living God."
- "Lord, half my goods I give to the poor."
- "I once was blind, now I see."

We have all these expectations, and we have Jesus. I'm saying to stick with Jesus and his way: The dead are raised, and the poor have good news brought to them. Stick with Jesus; jail or no jail; job or no job; health or sickness; young or old; pain or pleasure. Stick with Jesus. Now, where did we put that cross?

18

A Christmas Witness

December 19, 2010

Matthew 1:18–25

Matthew has a story for us. The theologian and ethicist Stanley Hauerwas says, "Matthew is training disciples" to know that the salvation delivered in the cross is different from the world's understanding of salvation. Salvation in Jesus does not depend on having power over enemies. We need this training because our addiction to worldly power makes it hard for us to grasp that our salvation does not come from the world and its power.

Our story has been so Americanized and secularized that is hard to tell what is fake and what is real. At one level this sermon attempts to tell the difference between the fake and the real.

Christmas has been victimized by sentimentalism, packed with secular images, deconstructed, and mangled out of recognition by well-meaning scholars. I don't want conservatives over-literalizing the story, and I don't want liberals telling me all the details that can't possibly be literally true. I want the Christmas story to be more majestic and more powerful.

All great stories have a beginning, so let's start there—Matthew 1:1–18: "An account of the genealogy of Jesus the messiah, the son of David, the son of Abraham." David was king, and Abraham was commanded by God to sacrifice his only Son, Isaac, whom he loved. Matthew teaches us that this king will end up on a cross—a king dragged out of the city bearing a cross, not a king riding in victory into the city raising a sword. Jesus is to be a different kind of king, a unique, only-one-of-his-kind king. This is our story—sparse, original, counter to everything we know about the world. Miss this, and we miss the whole story, and our Christianity becomes a pale imitation of the kingdom of God—a nationalistic idol.

Matthew's story begins with a family tree (1:2–18). "That's some family you got there, Jesus." Some R-rated, others X-rated. The Dominican philosopher Herbert McCabe suggests that in this genealogy, Matthew reminds us that Jesus was tied to the squalid reality of human life. Somehow, God used people whose very lives were opposed to the ways of God to accomplish the ways of God. Isn't it striking that the ways of God are not some house of cards that can be cast aside by some garden-variety punk king or half-baked bunch of enemies?

Look at these people: Rahab, the prostitute of Jericho. Tamar, the widow who dressed as a prostitute and tricked her father-in-law into having sex. The wife of Uriah—Bathsheba—the mother of Solomon. That's just the women in the list. They make *Desperate Housewives* look like a Brownie troop. And the men—well, this is the list for women who are attracted to bad boys: Jacob—liar, cheater, and thief of his own brother; in cahoots with his own mother to deceive his own father. David—king through intrigue and murder. Solomon—young king known as the wisest of men finally driven into paganism by 700 wives. How do we manage to get bent out of shape when the church is still filled with the same kind of people—passionate, ordinary, mistake-riddled, hard-trying people? "This is some family we have."

Our story is a mixed bag of the wholesomely human and the devilishly corrupt in us —and I'm sticking to it.

At the end of the long list there is Joseph—a righteous young man engaged to Mary. Matthew tells us that Joseph finds out that Mary is pregnant, but the two of them haven't had sex. Joseph, a thoughtful man, decides to break off the engagement quietly in order to avoid public disgrace.

Of all things, Joseph dreams of Mary, and an angel drops in: "Mary is going to have a baby, Joseph, and you are to name him Jesus. And this is the Holy Spirit's doings." Imagine Joseph later saying, "Mary, I dreamed about you last night." The plot gets richer. Ah, this is our story.

Now, Joseph had every right to divorce Mary, but he chose not to exercise his rights. Joseph doesn't care about rights; he loves Mary. He makes all men look good for a moment: empathy, compassion, understanding. A real man.

Our story is not about rights. Every time an American waves his Bible or his copy of the Constitution, I pray, "God, have mercy on America." We have so much trouble with the story in American Christianity. We keep mixing the American story with the Christmas story of Jesus. There's this guy named David Barton, who is not a historian but pretends to be one in front of large groups of conservative Christians. He has this fake story where he claims that the Declaration of Independence is a compilation of evangelical sermons. His version is so blatantly anti-historical that you might as well put George Washington and Thomas Jefferson in the manger and have Jesus grow up saying, "Give me liberty or give me death," instead of, "The Son of man has come to suffer and to die."

This strange mixed drink of American Christianity with Christmas leads to all kinds of other distortions. For example, some Christians are losing sleep over the alleged conspiracy to take Christ out of Christmas. Most of this argument centers in the use of "Happy Holidays" instead of "Merry Christmas" and those suspect signs "Merry Xmas." Do you really think that powerful corporate executives get together to strategize about ways to take Christ out of Christmas? Wall Street CEO's do get together for breakfast, according to a recent article in The New York Times, but they are certainly not worrying about Christ in or out of Christmas. They discuss derivatives, safeguard their multitrillion-dollar market, defend their dominance, fight government regulation, and try to block other banks from entering the market. They are worrying about what will be in their Christmas stockings—huge bonuses; not about Jesus Christ.

In Tulsa, Oklahoma, not exactly the citadel of liberal conspiracy, the City Council voted to change the name of its Christmas parade to Holiday Parade of Lights. As a result, a prominent Baptist preacher put the Tulsa City Council on the "Grinch List"—equivalent to the terrorist watch list.

One more example should suffice: In cities across America, various atheist groups are using billboards and signs on city buses to promote their message. "Millions of people are good without God." Some Christians rented a sign truck to follow the city bus. Their sign reads: "God is love: Two and a half billion people are good with God."

One preacher said, "I just don't think it should be on public transportation." The same preachers who want the Ten Commandments posted on federal buildings, Nativity scenes in malls, prayers at public events, and Christian symbols mixed with national ones in public, are now claiming they don't want atheists using the same public arena to promote their message. Is public advertising for Christians only?

This doesn't mean that we have no real enemies. The original villain of Christmas is Herod. Herod told the wise men he wanted to go and worship the child, but he wanted to kill the child. Herod even signed an executive order to kill all the male babies in Bethlehem.

Our literature is filled with enemies of Christmas, and these fictional characters have more substance than the fake enemies of the campaign to take Christ out of Christmas, or the atheists who don't want to feel alone in the world. My favorite fictional Christmas enemy is the Grinch:

> You're a mean one, Mr. Grinch
> You really are a heel.
> You're as cuddly as a cactus ...
> The three best words that best describe you are as follows, and I quote:
> Stink.
> Stank.
> Stunk!

Relax: You can't stop Christmas. As long as there are people willing to gather and sing with the angels, "Joy to the World, the Lord is come," there will be Christ in Christmas. Did you see the YouTube video of the flash mob in a food court blasting out the "Hallelujah Chorus" from Handel's *Messiah*?

But the real enemies of Christmas are no laughing matter. Christians raised on the primary metaphor "life is war" often make up enemies—enemies easy to despise, easier yet to criticize, and easiest of all to feel smugly superior to and then fight. Too much that passes for Christian witness is nothing more than smoke from the pulpit of The First Church of Huff and Puff.

Here's the deal: When real enemies show up, there is real persecution. There's a murmuring among American Christians that they are being persecuted. Some Christians feel something is being taken from them. They even think that someone stole the country from them, and they are now in the process of taking it back. Steal a whole country? Where would you hide it?

This sense of loss is real, but it is not a cause for grief. We are not losing the Christian faith; we are losing our cultural version of the Protestant faith. American Christians are not being persecuted. Criticized? Sure. We deserve it. We are not a perfect bunch. Made fun of? Of course. We are funny people. But persecuted? No. More prayer and less paranoia, please.

Here are a few incidents of real persecution: Terrorists invaded a Christian church in Iraq and gunned down 69 people. The Christian community in Iraq is migrating to Kurdish territory. A Protestant pastor in Vietnam was beaten unconscious by Ho Chi Minh City officials and his Bible school bulldozed. Two Baptist pastors in Russia were fined after their congregations sang Psalms and spoke about Christ in the streets. In Iran, a pastor has been sentenced to death for his faith in Jesus Christ. A woman in Pakistan offered a bowl of water to a group of women farm workers suffering in the heat. Her water was rejected as unclean because she is a Christian. After she defended her faith in a conversation, she was arrested and sentenced to death for blasphemy. That is persecution.

There is only one appropriate Christian response: real witness.

If we are serious about keeping Christ in Christmas, we have to learn that we are witnesses to a whole new world and not slaves to our American culture. Christmas witnesses had better not cry and had better not pout. This requires, as James McClendon insists, "a revised engagement with those still [fixated] on the culture of origin." Unless we are engaged in transmitting our story and being transformed by its power, through mutual repentance, we cannot be a community of witness commissioned by the risen Christ. Our own repentance is our only hedge against degenerating into hard-nosed moralists, soft-headed pietists, or pigheaded rationalists. Christmas requires witnesses, not moral police, pious judges, or rationalist scholars.

Let us not be deterred by fake enemies and fake persecution; let us not settle for fake witness. 'Tis the season for Christians to offer witness to the birth of the one we revere and serve as our savior, lord, and king—Jesus the messiah, son of David, son of Abraham.

This is our story. And oh, did I tell you? I'm sticking to it.

19

Would You Like to Hold the Baby?

December 24, 2010

Isaiah 9:1–9, Luke 2:1–20

CREATION WAS THE FIRST Christmas—all the gifts of God poured out on a fragile but astounding ecosystem called Earth.

> In the beginning,
> the earth was a formless void with darkness.
> Then God said, "Let there be light"; and there was light.

Millions of lights from millions of galaxies. Gifts of beauty. The joy of aliveness. Make no mistake Creation was Christmas.

John, whose gospel has no manger narrative, narrates Christmas for philosophers and theologians. After all, we need Christmas too. What came into being:

> In him was life, and the life was the light of all people.
> The light shines in the darkness, and the darkness did not overcome it. (John 1:4–5)

James Autry, in his poem "Christmas," says that every Christmas in their little country church in Mississippi, the preacher asked them to keep the spirit of Christmas all year long, and they always promised to try. And so it goes, year after year—all of us trying, failing, and at times getting it right. It's Christmas.

Imagine millions of years without a Christmas. Darkness and cold and death as if the White Witch of Narnia had cursed the land. After the disaster in the garden, where God's gifts were trashed and discarded faster than our children ripping open presents under the tree, humankind became the hopeless kind. Then a couple named Abram and Sarai, in their old age, were given a son—Isaac, all the promise in the world. His name means laughter. God must have laughed out loud at this move, and I think it sounded like the laugh of James Earl Jones.

Imagine all those centuries of slavery in Egypt. Moses thundered, "Let my people go," and the people who walked in chains saw a great light of liberation.

Disaster piled on disaster like clods of dark dirt falling on a casket. In all those dark centuries, God is passing out the gifts: a small ark atop treacherous waves; a rainbow in the sky; manna and water in the wilderness; words on twin tablets; a land of promise flowing with milk and honey; a temple, priests, kings, and prophets.

There's a bumper sticker that asks, "How's that hopey changey thing working out for you?" I would like to answer the question posed by this tacky saying that now passes for political narrative: "We rejoice in our sufferings, knowing that suffering produces endurance, and endurance produces character, and character produces hope, and hope does not disappoint us, because God's love has been poured into our hearts through the Holy Spirit" (Romans 5:3–5). "If anyone is in Christ, he is the New Creation, the old has passed away, behold the new has come" (2 Corinthians 5:17). The air in Bethlehem was thick with hope and change.

Finally Christmas came to a small town named Bethlehem—a town often associated with burial rather than birth. A trio of faithful women is associated with Bethlehem. Rachel died while giving birth to Benjamin on the road to Bethlehem (Genesis 35:19). But Bethlehem was also the place of new beginnings for Ruth, a foreigner, a Moabite, who came to town with Naomi, her mother-in-law. Remember her affirmation of faith: Your people shall be my people, and your God my God. Where you die, I will die—there will I be buried" (Ruth 1:16–17).

But we have a problem. Scripture passes out harsh judgment on Moab: No Moabite shall enter the assembly of the Lord; because they did not meet you with bread and with water on the way, when you came forth out of Egypt" (Deuteronomy 23:3–4). But here's Ruth, a Moabite, in Bethlehem, married to Boaz. Ruth gives birth to a son, and the women of Bethlehem name him Obed; the father of Jesse, the father of David, and at long last, Jesus, of the house and lineage of David. Unto us a child is given. Somewhere, Lewis Thomas, in his list of the seven modern wonders of the world, says that wonder No. 1 is a human child, born anywhere in the world. Wonder upon wonder.

What a message for Christmas: The judgment of Scripture can be invalidated by progressive revelation or a new understanding of the ways of God. This land belongs to the Prince of Peace, and no judgment is final. No outsider is left outside forever. Bethlehem has become the city of grace and truth. Christmas is the New Creation.[1] And we could use a New Creation.

Bethlehem—birth and burial. Luke Timothy Johnson says that the phrasing in Luke 2—"wrapped him in cloth strips, placed him in a manger, because there was no place"—matches the phrasing Luke 23, "wrapped him in linen cloth, placed him in a rock-hewn tomb, where no one had yet been laid." Birth and death mirror each other. "Christ was born, Christ has died, Christ is risen, Christ will come again."

Mary and Joseph didn't shuffle off to Bethlehem to sit by a lake and watch the world go by.[2] They were summoned by an emperor who needed more taxes. Somehow it also seems to be about politics, but we only think it's about politics because we trust God too little. The empire deals in taxes and death, but God delivers gifts of life and salvation.

What happened? Mary gave birth to her firstborn son. Let Rachel and Ruth rejoice. There was an ancient prophecy of Rachel weeping for her children because they were not (Jeremiah 31:15), but Rachel weeps no more. She died on the road to Bethlehem, but Mary now delivers the Christmas that the world had longed for and waited for, the day the world most needed but didn't know it needed. "For to us a child is born, to us a son is given; and the government shall be upon his shoulder." Upon us a light shines. Our joy is increased, not just by gifts under a tree, but by the gifts of God for the people of God.

Our God was born a homeless infant; we see him wrapped in the arms of Mary and hear him cry for the first time from a wood-carved manger. Can we see now why the Catholics call her mother of God? Thirty-three years later, Jesus would tell the mothers of Jerusalem, "Weep not for me but for your children," because he saw the insanity of violence grip his people. And then the cry, "My God, my God, why have you forsaken me?" as he died on a cross, homeless as the day he was born. Born in the back yard, killed outside the city, buried in a borrowed tomb. "Let us then go to him outside the camp and bear the abuse he endured. For here we have no lasting city, but we are looking for the city that is to come" (Hebrews 13:13–14). We are all homeless, but heaven is around the corner.

"Wrapped in swaddling cloths": Jesus is the Christmas gift. I can't explain how the magnificence of God was poured into an infant weighing maybe seven pounds: The one who laid the foundation of the earth now lying in a manger; the one who determined the measurements of an ever-expanding universe now a tiny baby; the one who shut in the sea with doors, made clouds its garment, and thick darkness its swaddling band now wrapped in swaddling cloths; the maker of galaxies now held in the arms of a young girl.

If not for some shepherds, watching their flock by night, this event would have passed under the radar of our world of power politics. Shepherds, bottom rung of the ladder, received heaven's invitation: "Be not afraid; for behold, I bring you good news of a great joy which will come to all the people; for to you is born this day in the city of David a Savior, who is Christ the Lord."

Before the shepherds can catch their breath, "There was with the angel a multitude of the heavenly host praising God and saying, 'Glory to God in the highest, and on earth peace among humans with whom he is pleased.'" The angels had been practicing this piece of music for millennia to sing it only this one time. Luke makes it clear that we are the ones who have to learn to sing it for the world to hear. The shepherds scurry off to Bethlehem representing the church. Is Luke telling us that the day is coming when there will be a multitude of the human host praising God? Well, listen to this: "Then I heard what seemed to be the voice of a great multitude, like the sound of many waters and like the sound of mighty thunderpeals, crying, "Hallelujah! For the Lord our God reigns!"

"The government shall be upon his shoulders!"

Now, take one last peek at that manger. Mary gently lifts Jesus from the crib, holds him in her arms, and with a trusting smile asks the only question that really matters: "Would you like to hold the baby?"

Let me ask you, "Would you like to hold the baby?" Reach out your arms. Now, open heart and mind and spirit to hold him forever. Ah, now it is Christmas.

ENDNOTES

1. Following John Yoder, I capitalize New Creation.
2. Thank you, John Fogarty.

20

Remember Your Baptism

JANUARY 9, 2011

Matthew 3:13–17

> When Jesus came to Jordan
> to be baptized by John,
> he did not come for pardon.

JESUS DIDN'T HAVE TO be baptized. Baptism was for sinners, and Jesus was not a sinner. The idea no longer shocks us because we have absorbed all those psychological lessons about why Jesus was baptized, like Jesus not knowing he was the Messiah. Please put me down as one who believes that Jesus knew.

And Matthew knew, because Matthew begins the ministry of Jesus with baptism (3:13–17) and concludes the ministry of Jesus with the command for us to go baptize all people (28:18–20). It's a Gospel wrapped in baptism. So why did Jesus submit to baptism?

A core teaching of our faith is that he did it as and for Israel and for us. Christians, for example, have always held that Isaiah 53 should be applied to Jesus. Surely he was wounded for our transgressions. Carlyle Marney says that when the doctor picks up the chart to diagnose the patient, the doctor discovers that he is the one afflicted, wounded, crushed, and bruised.

This adds meaning to Isaiah 42's servant of God: A bruised reed he will not break, and a dimly burning wick he will not quench. Every time a bunch of Christians go into mean-spirited mode, before they take a vote, they should read these words. We would have to be blind not to see how many bruised reeds and dimly burning wicks and burned-out stumps and broken hearts live among us. If you doubt that, then look at the line queuing up for baptism—there in the middle of all those people needing a second chance. There—see the straight-backed, dark-skinned one, waiting his turn? That's our Jesus, and he went into the water for all of us: "Let my people go."

We should not deceive people about the meaning of baptism or diminish its deep meaning (Baptist pun intended). A cross rises out of the water and makes a horizontal beeline to Jerusalem. And Jesus follows. Baptism is a journey of death and resurrection.

Matthew tells us that the baptism is the coronation of Jesus as king of the world. The key words are at the end of the story: "This is my Son, the Beloved, with whom I am well pleased." In a world riddled with insecure people, what more powerful words could be uttered? For every person who has longed to hear a father say, "You are my daughter, and I am so proud of you," this is really good news. Abba, Father, God, has called you by name and welcomed you as his daughter. While we are desperate for the approval of other people, Jesus receives divine approval. We already know what other people thought of him: "Isn't this the son of Joseph the carpenter?" Other people cut and hurt with unbending, mindless criticism. Remarks are snide and offhanded, but still they sting. But at his baptism, Jesus heard the only words that mattered: "This is my Son."

I pray for the day when the church will recover her sense of who she is and her pride in being a people of God. In the *Dallas Morning News*, I read a story about a meeting in the 1980s when the college football bowl presidents—there were only five then, not the current thirty-five—were discussing adding sponsors to their games. Finally, someone asked the longtime Cotton Bowl ambassador, "What do you think?" He said, "Gentlemen, I can just tell you this. If you ask somebody to buy your fiddle, they'll tell you what tunes to play." Well, an insecure church—desperate for worldly approval—has sold our fiddle to the world, and it tells us what tunes to play. The church needs to stop fiddling the world's tunes and go back to figuring out how to go forth teaching and baptizing the world.

Baptism is not a cute ritual for babies or a free ticket to heaven for pre-adolescents. It is far more than that, and Baptists, of all people, ought to lead the way in making sure people know that baptism is the entrance into the valley of the shadow of death, the long walk into the light and the Promised Land. I asked you to remember your baptism this morning. Touch, feel, renew your vows. Baptism is a really big deal.

So write this down: Jesus, not needing baptism, did it for us. He did it for the cause. One day, he was the carpenter of Nazareth, making yokes for oxen that fit well. After baptism, he is the Christ, the son of the living God, the king of the world. From the Jordan River to Calvary is a straight shot—an expressway of following God's will. We give the newly baptized a lighted candle; we should give them a cross, the belt of truth, the breastplate of righteousness, the shoes of peace, the shield of faith, the helmet of salvation, and the sword of the Spirit—the entire armor of God.

Matthew tells us that Jesus came from his home in Nazareth to be baptized by John in the Jordan. Baptism is a journey. The first Christians were called "people of the way." When James McClendon wrote his systematic theology as a Baptist, he chose "the way" as our primary understanding of the Christian life. "Follow, follow, I will follow Jesus."

Jesus is on a journey. Mary and Joseph journeyed to Bethlehem and Egypt and returned to Nazareth to live afterwards. They made a journey to Jerusalem when Jesus was twelve, and he announced, "I must be about my Father's business." And now 18 years later, the journey continues.

We have no idea what Jesus encountered in the long walk from the safety of Nazareth to the River Jordan, but we can trace his steps on a map of Israel. Jesus made his way down through the valley of Jezreel to the Jordan River. Jezreel Valley has served as the burial ground of kings and their violent armies across the centuries. There's King Saul committing suicide on Mount Gilboa, on the southeastern ridge of Jezreel. There's the rumbling chariot of Jehu "driving like a mad man" on his way to killing the kings of Israel and Judah because of the greedy, murderous reign of Jezebel and Ahab. At the opposite end of Jezreel sits Armageddon (Megiddo)—where legend has it that all the armies of the world will gather for a final battle between good and evil. This valley has been pocked with the spikes of warrior boots for centuries. Jesus is on his way to becoming the king who will put an end to the world's propensity for violence. Mary Oliver, in her poem "The Journey":

> One day you finally knew
> what you had to do, and began,
> though the voices around you
> kept shouting
> their bad advice—

> though the whole house
> began to tremble
> and you felt the old tug
> at your ankles.
> "Mend my life!"
> each voice cried.
> But you didn't stop.
> You knew what you had to do,
> though the wind pried
> with its stiff fingers
> at the very foundations—
> though their melancholy
> was terrible.
> It was already late
> enough, and a wild night,
> and the road full of fallen
> branches and stones.
> But little by little,
> as you left their voices behind,
> the stars began to burn
> through the sheets of clouds,
> and there was a new voice,
> which you slowly
> recognized as your own,
> that kept you company
> as you strode deeper and deeper
> into the world,
> determined to do
> the only thing you could do—
> determined to save
> the only life you could save.

There are two major differences for Jesus: He responded not to his own voice but to the voice of God, and he was determined to save not himself, but every life in the world.

Why does Jesus do this? Perhaps all that truth Mary had pondered in her heart she had poured into the heart of Jesus, and he now has learned what he has to do. Jesus tells us that he undergoes baptism because "It is right to do all that God requires." Perhaps the voice of Micah whispers to Jesus: "He has told you what is good; and what does the Lord require of you but to do justice, and to love kindness, and to walk humbly with your God?"

Baptism is a journey of doing all that God requires. American Christians have a hangup: We claim a status instead of a calling; we claim rights instead of requirements and privileges instead of responsibilities. Some Christians think they are morally superior and go about the business of cramming their moralism down everyone else's throat. Some Christians think they are emotionally superior and feel sorry for those who don't get carried away in worship. Some Christians think they are intellectually superior and delight in insulting the faith of those they deem ignorant. Some Christians think they are biblically superior and have been given special revelation. Some Christians think they are politically superior and we are in real trouble when a morally superior person is also afflicted with the illusion of political superiority.

Will Campbell says, "Everybody has to have someone they feel superior to." Jesus bursts the illusion of superiority in his baptism. See Jesus, our Jesus, baptized with sinners, reprobates, and failures. I can't help but see Flannery O'Connor's description of the swinging bridge to heaven populated by battalions of freaks and lunatics. What good news for all of us morally, culturally, economically, and politically inferior who carry insecurity with us from childhood like an old blanket without which we can't sleep.

Baptism, then, is a one-word language for the whole of our life of faith. The water ritual isn't repeated, but our baptism keeps happening. Some of us would be good people if there were someone there every day to baptize us, to figuratively immerse us in the water again. Let your morning prayer be, "Thank God I am baptized. I am baptized."

But wait: Jesus gave us a way to remember our baptism that our Baptist founders missed or dismissed. My grandmother's people, the Primitive Baptists, known affectionately as "Hard Shell Baptists," practice foot washing. In John 13, Jesus says, "So if I, your Lord and Teacher, have washed your feet, you also ought to wash one another's feet."

Rowan Williams says, "The church is the community of those who have been 'immersed' in Jesus's life."

Are we immersed, every day, in the life of Jesus? Well, here again is the good news: We are baptized. We belong to God. We're members of the church. God has said, "Behold, you are my son and my daughter, and with you I am well pleased." We are marked with the sign of the cross and the seal of the Holy Spirit. We know what is required of us—that we stay on the journey, that we be found faithful to our baptismal vows.

People of the living God, remember your baptism.

21

The World's Savior and America's Prophet

Dr. Martin Luther King Jr. Sunday

JANUARY 16, 2011

John 1:29–41

This Martin Luther King Jr. Sunday, the Gospel for today is "Behold the Lamb of God." Consider America's prophet and the world's true Savior: What's the connection?

The political powers hounded Jesus and crucified him; King was assassinated. "Behold the Lamb of God," cried John the Baptist. "We still have a choice today: nonviolent coexistence or violent co-annihilation," preached King.

The roots of that choice are found in our text. John the Baptist points a finger at Jesus and declares, "Behold, the Lamb of God." This changes everything. The entire ministry of Jesus now has a permanent mascot: a lamb. An early Byzantine painting shows a stick cross, and hanging there is a huge lamb.

Do you see what this means? This is not just any lamb; this is the lamb of nonviolence. Most New Testament scholars believe that the Lamb is the suffering servant of Isaiah and the paschal lamb sacrificed in the Temple. Time for biblical memory drill: Scripture says that Jesus *tabernacled* (a temple term) among us, that he is the mercy seat—the place in the temple where the blood of lambs was sprinkled; that he was like a lamb that is led to the slaughter. Remember Isaac, hands tied, lying on a makeshift altar of wood sticks, and over to the side stands a white lamb, waiting. "God will provide."

Did you know that Jesus was condemned to death at noon on the day before the Passover, and this was the exact time when the priests began to slay the paschal lambs in the Temple? Did you know that none of the bones of Jesus were broken on the cross, and that no bone of the paschal lamb was ever to be broken? "Christ our Passover has been sacrificed," says Paul in 1 Corinthians 5:7. Jesus is the nonviolent lamb of sacrificial love. Forget symbols of worldly power and violence. Our symbol is the Lamb of God. And this lamb is the temple of God.

Look, this metaphor has creative power. In fact, I argue that it has reality-producing power because it creates a reality different from the world: a lamb, not an elephant or a donkey; a lamb, not a fox; a lamb, not a goat.

Poet Mary Oliver writes, "If there's a temple, I haven't found it yet. I simply go on drifting, in the heaven of the grass and the weeds." Well, according to the Gospel, Jesus is the temple we have all been seeking: the temple of God, the temple of peace and wholeness. Somewhere in all of us there is the deep-seated need to experience God, the desire for the vision of Isaiah: I saw the Lord, and his glory filled the temple. And according to John, Jesus is the Temple we all seek.

The Gospels indicate that Jesus chose the way of nonviolence—the sword over the cross. "He could have called twelve legions of angels, but he went to the cross." Our problem in America is that rather than actually believing in Jesus, we believe in believing. Theologian and ethicist Stanley Hauerwas says, "Americans do not have to believe in God, because they believe that it is a good thing simply to believe: all they need is a general belief in belief. The god most Americans say they believe in . . . is only the god who guarantees them life, liberty, and wealth."

I ask you to believe something specific—that Jesus is the nonviolent Lamb of God.

"As Christians, we must maintain that peace is a gift of God that comes only by our being a community formed around a crucified savior—a savior who teaches us how to be peaceful in a world in rebellion against its true Lord," Hauerwas wrote in his book *The Peaceable Kingdom*. At very least, it means that the church must make sure that peace has a place at the table of nations, that even if you personally believe in war, you want your preacher to speak for peace.

King was one of God's sacrificial lambs. King preached that we should be governed by our dreams and not our fears. Tell that to the fear mongers populating the halls of Congress and the television studios. King preached that gentleness takes more courage than violence. How many are ready to be that courageous? King preached that compassion is more valuable than any ideology (William Sloane Coffin Jr.).

We can't claim to follow Jesus by worshipping the gods of war and the shrine of "national security." It is time to end the badly named war on terrorism and wage peace with bread, medicine, and education. "Love your enemies" is not optional advice for casual believers. "Beloved, never avenge yourselves" means never.

Our nation must break its addiction to being entertained by violence. Our political process has become "a shoddy, unplanned city that looks like it killed all its architects before it approved a master plan for its construction" (Pat Conroy, *My Reading Life*). Rather than attempting to take superficial advantage of every crisis, of using and manipulating and demeaning people, we have to once again find that common ground rooted in a spirit of peacefulness. Rather than ranting and spewing emotionally based charges, we have to reject the ruminations of disrespect that pollute our national dialogue. Sure, it is sad to hear people defend the low-road rhetoric in America, but people find it entertaining. They have little interest in our national character—only interest in the characters that populate our airwaves.

Of course, there's too much violence in America. Someone needs to once again teach us the gospel of nonviolence. King was my first teacher of the gospel of nonviolence, followed by Will Campbell; William Sloane Coffin Jr. and his campaign for nuclear disarmament; John Yoder, Anabaptist theologian; William McClendon, Baptist theology professor; and Hauerwas, especially his work, *The Peaceable Kingdom*.

What happened in Tucson, Arizona, on January 8, 2011, reminds us that violence is a form of madness. But we can't make a scapegoat of one mad shooter and pretend that he is the caricature of our opponents. The young man who critically wounded U.S. Representative Gabrielle Giffords and killed six others that fateful day doesn't represent who we are as Americans. I believe our national character is still strong because there are so many good people. This is not a time to silence dissent. Please dissent with passion, precision, and persuasive argument. Dissent until content, but do so with dignity and respect. Argue the details, the facts, and the evidence. Stay away from propaganda, deception, and lies. Winston Churchill said, "A lie goes halfway around the world before truth can get its pants on."

A good argument stands on a tripod: logic, character, and emotion. We have lost the art of arguing. (I believe there is a book worth writing around this theme of argument being reduced to emotion while elevating demagoguery.) American argument is now a middle-school food fight: Throw everything, and hope something nasty sticks. Emotion, intended as a supporting character to logic and character, has taken over the drama. It's not so much the bad language as it is the sheer vacuity of the pathetic words that now pass for argument that we should bemoan. I am not making a moralistic attack on common profanity. I'm referring to our loss of logic and character/credibility—logos and pathos. (God bless you, Aristotle.)

We all bear responsibility for the excessive emotionalism of our culture: rudeness, blatant exaggerations, caricatures of our opponents, out-of-control arrogance, and refusal to listen to one another. Attacking a person's character is not argument; it is an assassination.

This country needs more lambs and fewer wolves, foxes, and skunks. There are rules for the behavior of lambs: "Let love be genuine; hate what is evil, cling to what is good; love one another with brotherly affection; outdo one another in showing honor. Live in harmony with one another; do not be haughty."

Oh, it is not easy to be a sheep of God's pasture in a world of wolves. Wolves, by nature, still devour lambs as they did Jesus and King. Yet as God's lambs, we are not being sent unarmed into the world. Our armor is "lambware": the belt of truth, the breastplate of righteousness, the shoes of peace, the shield of faith, the helmet of salvation, and the sword of the Spirit. Onward, Lambs of God!

22

Are We Actually Following Jesus?

JANUARY 23, 2011

Matthew 4:12–23

As a child, I loved the hymn, *Follow, Follow, I Will Follow Jesus*. Like Mary's little lamb, anywhere that Jesus went, I was sure to follow. One day, it dawned on me that my Jesus never went anywhere except to church and back home again. He insisted that we go to church at least three times a week, especially on Sunday night, no matter how badly we wanted to stay home and watch *Bonanza*.

Our Jesus was white, really angry about civil rights, supportive of the KKK, a believer in guns, and opposed to seminary education, but he loved dinner on the ground, all-day singing, and protracted meetings. He read only the King James Version of the Holy Bible, and he insisted every word, comma, and period, including the chapter and verse number, was literal. He didn't like Catholics—even though there wasn't a single Catholic in our entire community. He didn't care for Germans or Japanese because of World War II. He was a big believer in hell and was always on the lookout for anyone smoking, drinking, or dancing. Unlike the Methodists, who had Coke and cookies at their Vacation Bible School, my stern Baptist Jesus believed in Nabisco saltine crackers and Kool-Aid.

Only later did I realize that most of us follow some image of Jesus we have concocted in our minds. It's as if there were a Build-A-Jesus store in the mall, and we get to make our own Jesus. I had no idea that I was living out the philosopher Fuerbach's claim that religion is the projection of mankind's hopes written large. And I also didn't realize how superficial it was. A self-made Jesus turns out to be a sorry building project.

The question before us today: Are we actually following Jesus? Let's put it this way: The church needs more than a GPS if we are going to really follow Jesus.

One day, Jesus came walking by the sea and said, "Follow me." Andrew, Peter, James, and John decided to attach their fate to the passionately humble teacher. The persuasiveness of Jesus hung in the air with an authenticity that was beyond criticism.

Since the fishermen immediately left their boats and followed Jesus, we can assume they felt "the strong attraction of a good man's gravitational pull." Over the next three years, these veteran fishermen would watch Jesus pull others into "his orbit as gracefully as a fly fisherman casting toward a still pool in a cold mountain stream" (Pat Conroy, *My Reading Life*).

Then of all things, Jesus says, "I will make you fishers of men and women." Following Jesus means being his witnesses.

"As Christians, we believe that peace is most perfectly realized as we learn to tell God's story," wrote Stanley Hauerwas in *The Peaceable Kingdom*. (We are, after all, a storytelling people.) Story creates tradition, and together, they create a community of faith. "Moreover," Hauerwas wrote, "God has charged us with the particular responsibility of being his representatives to attract others to that story of peace by manifesting it in our common life." It is both our privilege and responsibility to tell God's story.

The meaning of witness is telling the alternative story that this world is the creation of a good God who is known through the people of Israel and the life, death, and resurrection of Jesus Christ. "Without such a witness we only abandon the world to the violence derived from the lies that devour our lives" (Hauerwas).

If we don't keep telling the story and building the tradition, communities will fall apart.

Witnessing is not public grandstanding. The new governor of Alabama kicked up a storm in January 2011 by announcing that non-Christians were not his brothers and sisters. It was inappropriate and unnecessary. He apologized, but I remind Governor Robert Bentley that Jesus called the poor, the naked, the hungry, the prisoners, the sick, the lepers, the prostitutes, the robbers, and the tax collectors his brothers and sisters.

Are We Actually Following Jesus?   109

His remarks remind me of a college acquaintance standing on a table at a local restaurant and preaching at the top of his lungs. The manager threw us all out, even though I protested, "We weren't preaching; we came for the crawfish etouffee." Later, in a chapel service, my preacher pal interrupted a Baptist history professor's lecture on Baptist Heritage Day and shouted, "Excuse me, could you say something about Jesus?"

Such grandstanding is inappropriate whether expressed by naïve religious studies majors or seasoned political veterans. Christians should at least have good manners. After chapel, someone politely informed the preacher boy, "Jesus wouldn't treat a guest like that." People who disagree with fellow Christians are not pagans in need of prayer, heathens bound for hell, or socialists in need of salvation. As Soren Kierkegaard said, "Once you label me, you negate me."

Following Jesus also requires rigorous training. Jesus says, "I will make you." What a thought: We are "made" Christian men and women—not for a Mafia don but as disciples of the true savior of the world. That one phrase suggests the lifelong training necessary for discipleship. This is especially true of worship. "Because the Christian story is an enacted story, liturgy is probably a much more important resource than are doctrines or creeds" for training in discipleship. For example, that training will develop in us the capacity to love worship rather than be bored by it. Boredom is not a sign of poor preaching, although poor preaching may be a contributing factor. Boredom is the result of a lack of training in the skills of worship. In order for worship to be the single most important act of resistance to the power of evil, we must have our desires transformed, and that requires long training. And entertainment is not resistance. As Queen Victoria allegedly said, "If all the people who go to sleep in church were laid end to end, they would be a lot more comfortable."

Church members who wonder why they need training have never questioned why an untrained church shoots its own wounded. If all we need is to show up at church with a batch of private theological opinions picked up on religious television or the inadequate theology of a talk show host, we will not need skills for that. But if we want to sustain our faith and the church, we are going to need skills. None of us are as good at this as we need to be.

Discipleship training should be as intense as basic training for the military, as hard as practice for professional football players, as difficult as final exams for doctoral candidates. In the outrageous spoof *Knight and Day*, Tom Cruise keeps repeating to his co-star, "You have skills." Well, we must "develop disciplined skills through initiation into that community that attempts to live faithful to the story of God." For example, no one can just forgive enemies. It is self-serving for a preacher to smile indulgently and say, "Love your enemies," as if he were asking us to love our mothers. To love enemies is a high-level spiritual skill.

Jesus brought training and skills to his wilderness contest with evil far exceeding those of a Jedi warrior. Listen, you can't go one on one with the evil empire and survive without godly skills. Church casualty lists are heartbreaking. Nationwide, 1,600 ministers a month are forced to resign their pulpits. More than 60 percent of church members quit the church. We are a wounded, battered army with flags dragging in the dust like the scarred, emaciated ghosts of the Confederacy returning home. A certain kind of people is required to sustain the church over time—a people of character and virtue. We need skills. As Baptists, we have such a predisposed determination to be saved by grace alone that we have neglected training in the virtues. This may account for us having more characters than people with character.

We especially need skill with the Bible. The Bible invites argument and disagreement. Jacob bargains with God; Job argues with God; Jonah disagrees with God. If we think the Bible always agrees with us, then we are reading badly and interpreting wrongly. Frankly, there are texts in the Bible that should blow our minds. Reading this book should, at times, elicit from our lips:

- Forgive me, Lord, for I am a sinner.
- Lord, have mercy.
- Help my unbelief.

It could also elicit more down-to-earth expressions:
- Are you kidding me?
- Say it ain't so, Jesus.
- Or, as a Baptist deacon faced with Scripture's condemnation of racism said, "I don't care what the Bible says."

The Bible forces us to examine every facet of our lives and beliefs. We need Bible skills.

Following Jesus means serving the constituency that Jesus served. We can call this practical service: feeding the hungry, giving water to the thirsty, welcoming strangers, clothing the naked, caring for the sick, and visiting the prisoners. Here are six primary mission practices for Christian churches. Jesus healed people with unclean spirits, lepers, paralytics, a man with a withered hand, a man tortured by mental demons, the mentally diseased, sick and dying children, the blind, the lame, the deaf, and a boy with epilepsy. Do we get the picture? Following Jesus means serving Jesus's people.

Patience is a required virtue if we are to serve the needy people of Jesus. To follow Jesus is to have the skill to wait with him in a world of hunger, idolatry, and war. Following Jesus offers an alternative time to a world that believes we have no time to be just or that we can't afford to be just. We have the time to feed our neighbors and keep working on solutions to worldwide hunger, health care, and poverty. The hungry man with his hand out is our Jesus. The single mom needing health care for her children—she's our Jesus. There's all this need.

Following Jesus means faithful witness, rigorous training, and practical service. So, you tell me. Are we following Jesus?

23

How to Be Blessed

January 30, 2011

Matthew 5:1-12

The Beatitudes of Jesus are not the happy, sappy attitudes of the positive thinking crowd. They are for the broken, hurt, persecuted, sometimes down people of Christ.

Pat Conroy, in *My Reading Life,* describes his encounter with a high school librarian in Beaufort, South Carolina. With apologies to all wonderful librarians, I tell this story. Conroy writes, "For Miss Hunter . . . . the state of nirvana would be a library cleaned of all readers and the books all shelved and accounted for. She was famous for her need for absolute control of her book-lined fiefdom. She seemed agitated every time a student disturbed the airspace of her private domain. In the years I knew her, I never saw her reading a book or talking about a book she'd read. Her familiarity with literature was suspect, and she placed the Sherlock Holmes collection in the biography section."

Don't you think that church members can be like Miss Hunter? We can live among the people of Jesus, worship in his church, and have no organic relationship to who he is and what he teaches. But if we live anywhere in proximity to Jesus, we will have to face his primary teaching—the Beatitudes—and believe me, these are not hints for successful living or recommendations for the good life or the secrets to happiness, health, and wealth.

Make no mistake: Jesus is not setting up an impossible obstacle course for individuals; he's setting the agenda for his church. Private, personal, and pietistic readings of the Beatitudes lead to pride and frustration. Don't call this a list of requirements, but a picture of a real church. Don't call this a universal ethic that can be practiced with a little hard work and effort. Such a rendering of the Beatitudes leaves us where the church too often leaves folks: with a guilty feeling. For all of you trained from childhood in the fine art of feeling guilt and despising yourself, this sermon is for you.

The Beatitudes challenge us because they are aliens in our culture. Meekness, mercy, and peace—the language of church—are incomprehensible to the world.

Part of the reason: the Beatitudes are rooted in humility. Humility lives as an outcast in our arrogant world. Arrogance and self-righteousness own the souls of so many. Humility is a reticent, shy virtue. She refuses to go where she is not invited. No shrinking violet, and stronger than steel, she still waits to be invited on a date. Humility balks at raised voices, showoffs, swelled heads, or bad manners. Humility packs her bag and leaves the ARB church: The Always Right Baptists. Someone has said, "Being humble is like trying to catch air in your hands." A person becomes humble unconsciously while being faithful to Jesus Christ.

Humility and her children—the Beatitudes—are the path to blessing. Call it mission impossible, but as hard as it is, we are still called to live the Beatitudes. This is not an All-American tale of a lone cowboy taking on the world with six-shooters blazing. The church lives the Beatitudes together. The Beatitudes are, as theologian and ethicist Stanley Hauerwas puts it in *Matthew: Brazos Theological Commentary on the Bible*, "the constitution of a people. You cannot live by the demands of the [Beatitudes alone], and that is exactly the point."

The Beatitudes are a family photo of a people gathered by and around Jesus. Matthew says Jesus went up on the mountain, and his disciples came to him. Here is the real church—the followers of Jesus—listening and imitating him. Isn't this the best possible news? Jesus, the master of humility, is our teacher. Matthew 16:29:—"Take my yoke upon you, and learn from me; for I am gentle and humble in heart."

Listen, we can crank out Bach and Beethoven with full orchestra, we can preach like Elijah and Paul; we can even feed hungry people, but until the Beatitudes are our way of life, we are not the church Jesus intends. No one of us possesses all the Beatitudes, but wherever Jesus gathers disciples, Hauerwas writes, "we can be sure that some will be poor, some will mourn, and some will be meek."

Jesus offers up the Beatitudes as his response to our world's circle of violence. Have you seen the Allstate television ads with the character named Mayhem? Our world is populated with guys like him. They break, bruise, and batter everything and everyone in the world.

Violence is a way of relating that inflicts pain on all of life including the environment and all creatures. Treating another as inferior is a form of violence. Ask any child ever bullied on the playground. Ask any person ever threatened, intimidated, or beaten for just being different. In line at the supermarket, I saw a single mom with three children pay for her groceries with food stamps, and heard the low bitter murmuring of affluent customers. Was it envy of the poor, or just a deep-seated anger at the thought that someone might get something for nothing? So Jesus, looking at our world, offers us the Beatitudes as a gift, as a way of anti-violence. Practice the Beatitudes, and you will not participate in the violent ways of our world.

Yet there's no wonder we work so hard to mimic the world and to get ahead. The Beatitudes aren't good references on a resume. You can't say, "I will make a good investment banker because I am merciful, meek, and pure of heart."

Our grab-and-go world has neither the patience nor the wisdom to fit the Beatitudes into a busy schedule. From the first time we do or do not make the honor roll in first grade until the day we retire, we know the score. In a world of competition, we have to do something to stay one step in front. Our world has its own beatitudes, writes J.P. Phillips in *Your God Is Too Small:* "Happy are the pushers: for they get on in the world. Happy are the hard-boiled: for they never let life hurt them. Happy are they who complain: for they get their own way in the end. Happy are the blasé: for they never worry over their sins. Happy are the slave-drivers: for they get results. Happy are the big mouths: for they get on television and distort reality. Happy are the angry demagogues: they deceive people and rule with iron fists. Happy are the knowledgeable: for they know how to work the system. Happy are the troublemakers: for people have to take notice of them."

What's the answer? In a gathering storm of mayhem, the church has to load up on the virtues of the Beatitudes, because we church types are called to live the Beatitudes. Hauerwas writes in *The Peaceable Kingdom,*

"The goal of Christian living is to follow Jesus and to share with the other disciples in seeking the [peaceable kingdom] of God."

When we open our hands with gratitude to receive the gift of the Beatitudes from one another, we will find the hard edges of life dissipating, the tendencies to be judgmental and self-righteous shrink, and life is filled with blessings. The church looks really good wrapped in the Beatitudes.

And look, as if from nowhere, the manifold, multiple blessings of God appear. To us belongs the kingdom of God, the comfort of the Holy Spirit, and the inheritance of the earth. We shall be filled with righteousness and receive mercy and grace to help in our hour of need. We shall see God and be called children of God. We shall be the most blessed people on the face of this planet. And as we go about our Beatitude-practicing life, humility will quietly take up residence in our hearts, and we won't have to say anything. Others will see the light shining in our eyes. They will see the spirit of Jesus on our faces; the world will grow strangely dim, and the blessings of God will pour forth from the skies.

www.ingramcontent.com/pod-product-compliance
Lightning Source LLC
Chambersburg PA
CBHW071858160426
43197CB00013B/2520